Dedicated

To Everyone Who Ever Took a

Chance on God

for the Sake of Others

ABOUT THE COVER: When my boys were young, one of their favorite movies was Disney's animated classic "The Lion King." In one scene, Simba, the young and precocious son of King Mufasa, steps into a paw imprint left by his much bigger and wiser father. The contrast is not lost on the young cat. Simba's paw seemed so small and insignificant compared to his father's. It was a powerful reminder to Simba that he had a lot of growing ahead before he would reach his potential and assume the mantle of king.

I think each one of us is like Simba. There is the person we currently are – and there is the person God has created us to become. When it comes to our God-given calling and spiritual giftedness, we must embrace the journey of growth that comes with reaching our potential. We must grow in our character, our competency, and our clarity.

Jesus was called the Lion of Judah (Revelation 5:5). We are called to be made new in his image (Romans 8:29). God is glorified when we follow Jesus and allow him to mold and grow us into little "lions of Judah." Your paw print may be small at the moment – but don't despair, growth will come as you walk with Jesus. Lion cubs are cute, but Lion Kings shape the world. Which will you choose?

Contents

Part 1

A Biblical Guide To Becoming Dangerous

Being Good Or Becoming Dangerous?

"Enemy occupied territory, that's what this world is. Christianity is the story of how the rightful king has landed, in disguise, and is calling us to a grand campaign of sabotage."

C.S. Lewis, Mere Christianity

Since 1919, the FBI has posted their famous WANTED posters in post offices across the United States.[1] All kinds of infamous criminals have earned their way onto those sheets of paper – haunting black and white images staring coldly at the countless innocent people just trying to send birthday cards and Christmas packages. I remember as a boy looking at one of those posters and feeling a fearful chill run down my spine.

These people were dangerous.

But what if we could flip the script and make being dangerous a good thing? What if aligning ourselves to the heart of God, and his plan for everything, made you dangerous in a good way ... in ALL the right ways?

What if there was a post office in Hell that featured WANTED posters of these kinds of people?

Would the inhabitants of Hell look upon those posters and feel fear? More importantly, would your picture be among the haunting images reminding Hell's minions that their time was running out?

What if aligning your hopes, fears, dreams, talents, training, passions, and even your pain with God made you dangerous in the eyes of Satan.

Do you fear Satan? Or does Satan fear you?
The reality should be the latter. Too often it is the former.

---

1 | At the time it was called the Bureau of Investigation, and the first poster featured a World War 1 deserter named William Bishop.

This is because we misunderstand some basic truths concerning the scriptures and the mission of Jesus. But we can change that ...

Invasion Not Evasion

*"And I tell you, you are Peter, and on this rock I will build my church, **and the gates of hell shall not prevail against it."**[2]*

Everyday church people often misinterpret these words. The metaphor Jesus is using is one of conflict. Too many times people default into thinking it is the church that is on the defensive in this passage.[3] But I ask you – whose gates is Jesus alluding to?

That's right ... it's Hell's gates.

Historically in ancient times the gates of a city were thought to be the weakest link in the walls of its defense. The walls of cities were often many meters thick, but the gates had to be movable enough to allow in travelers and commerce. This is why sieges were usually centered on the gates of cities. The gates were the natural place to conduct negotiations. But if those were unsuccessful, they were also the most strategic place to break through and win the battle.

Metaphor or not, when it comes to spiritual battle, the gates of Hell are likely quite formidable. But this does not deter Jesus from making an absolutely audacious claim: the gates of Hell will not be strong enough to withstand the invasion of the Kingdom of God. This is an invasion ordained by God and carried out by the Church.

But wait a minute. At this point in the story, just who is the "church"?[4]

Let's consider who it is not. It is not a massive movement of people. It is not breath-taking cathedrals or scores of monasteries. It is not an intimidating hierarchy of officials led by powerful popes and monarchs who can usher huge crusading armies at the whisper of command.

---

2 | Matthew 16:18

3 | It may be that people's impressions of spiritual warfare are more shaped by hymns like *Martin Luther's A Mighty Fortress Is Our God* than the actual biblical text.

4 | This is the first use of the word for church in scripture ekklesia (Greek meaning the gathered).

No ... at this point, the church is twelve guys who still aren't fully sure what the heck is going on. They are relatively uneducated, slow to understand, and often struggle to even get along with each other. They do not represent the cream of the crop if you were trying to recruit the core of what will be the single most important movement in history. This is most definitely NOT a spiritual version of Navy SEAL Team 6, and yet Jesus has no doubt about the outcome of this battle royal.

Though Jesus is fully aware that his time with these men and women was drawing to a close, he was also preparing them to receive what would be a secret weapon – the Holy Spirit. It would be this Spirit who would transform these very ordinary followers into dangerous ambassadors and who would serve as living signs of an approaching new reality.

You see, this is where so many Christians get the trajectory of scripture wrong. They believe Jesus appeared in order to die for our sins so we can eventually escape to heaven. But this interprets the plan of God exactly backwards. Jesus came to proclaim the coming Kingdom of God, not provide a manual on how to be good little boys and girls in the hopes that we might go to heaven.

The Gospels are about *invasion*, not evasion.

You doubt? Rethink some of these most well-known scriptures:

> *"Our Father who art in heaven, hallowed be thy name. Thy Kingdom **come**, thy will be done, **on earth as it is in heaven...**"*[5]

> *"The Spirit of the Lord is on me, he anointed me to proclaim good news for the poor, ... to proclaim freedom for the prisoners, to restore sight to the blind, to set the oppressed free and proclaim the year of the Lord's favor,"*[6]

> *"Blessed are the meek, for they shall inherit the earth ..."*[7]

C.S. Lewis was right – the story of Christianity is about how the rightful king has landed, in disguise, and is calling us to a grand

5 | Matthew 6:9-10
6 | Luke 4:18-19
7 | Matthew 5:5

campaign of sabotage. In Jesus Christ, God has come to reclaim, redeem, and renew that which was always his.

The Kingdom of God is covertly present and growing – even in the midst of evil, rebellion, and brokenness. This is why Jesus often described the Kingdom in ways that seemed quite humble.

> *"The kingdom of heaven is like a mustard seed, which a man took and planted in his field. Though it is the smallest of all seeds, yet when it grows, it is the largest of garden plants and becomes a tree, so that the birds come and perch in its branches."*

> *"He told them still another parable: "The kingdom of heaven is like yeast that a woman took and mixed into about sixty pounds of flour until it worked all through the dough."*[8]

The Kingdom of Heaven is like yeast ...

When I was in high school, I learned the hard way the secret, expansive power of yeast. One morning as I was hurriedly trying to get to my first class of the day (a 7:45 Physics class – uff da), I opened my locker expecting to grab my textbook and run. However, as I snapped the lock open and swung open the rattling door, my Physics textbook was nowhere to be seen. This was because the entire contents of my locker had been swallowed up in dough ... yes, as in bread dough. As best as I could tell, someone had gotten into my locker the evening prior, and put some bread dough in the upper compartment of my locker to rise over night. They must have used a lot of it because by the time I arrived on the scene, the dough had completely overwhelmed the contents on my locker.[9]

It was as if the Pillsbury Doughboy had been hired to carry out a hit on me. It was quite the practical joke. Yea .... it was really funny ... ha – ha.

---

8 | Matthew 13:31-33

9 | Only two people had my locker combination – my girlfriend (who is now my wife), and the cheerleader who was assigned to decorate my locker on basketball game days. To my shame, for the longest time I thought my girlfriend had conspired with my buddies to prank me, but even to this day, she denies it was her. Given that there is no reason for her to lie about it all these years later, I must conclude it was the cheerleader. So always remember ... never trust a cheerleader.

The bread dough was everywhere … sticking shut the covers of my notebooks, clogging the zipper of my jacket, even creeping into my gym bag (I'm not even going to get into what that looked like). The dough found its way into pages of all of my textbooks – all of the major academic disciplines had been invaded by the yeasty explosion.

I think this illustrates the nature of the invading Kingdom of God. The truth, knowledge, love, and grace of God in Christ Jesus is yeast-like in its expansion, permeating every nook and cranny of creation – seeking to reclaim and redeem all that was originally God's. Christians become dangerous in all the right ways when they bring the mind of Christ and their spiritual giftedness into science, mathematics, medicine, education, literature, the social sciences and the fine arts. In so doing, believers participate and become signs of the growing rule of God.

*Thy Kingdom come, Thy will be done **on earth** as it is in heaven.*

Ticket Holder or Kingdom Builder?

And so it comes down to a question of perspective.

If your understanding of the Gospel involves merely believing the right stuff so you can escape to heaven, then you are just a ticket holder. For you, the salvation afforded by the cross of Jesus is a commodity to be tucked away until you die, and then presented like a ticket for entrance into the big event. However, this renders your current life in the here and now with less meaning and purpose than it could have …

> • Why let God purge and heal you of your sinful nature now, if you get to go to heaven later? (I mean – really – that sounds painful and inconvenient.)

> • Why take risks for justice here if it's just about waiting to escape elsewhere? (Besides – standing up for justice tends to be a dangerous business.)

> • Why invest in the care of the environment if God is going to trash the current creation and start all over? (After all, this place isn't my home, I'm just passing through.)

This immature understanding makes your current life smaller – conforming it into something more like a waiting room than a battlefield – and that hardly satisfies the longings and intuitions of your heart, does it?

If you believe the Gospel is only about maintaining your status as a good boy or girl until you can escape to some ethereal heaven, then you have completely missed the point of God's grand story, and worse yet, misread the heart of God as revealed in Jesus.[10] The Apostle Paul wrote about the misplaced life focus of such Christians when he said,

> "For no one can lay any foundation other than the one already laid, which is Jesus Christ. If anyone builds on this foundation using gold, silver, costly stones, wood, hay or straw, their work will be shown for what it is, because the Day will bring it to light. It will be revealed with fire, and the fire will test the quality of each person's work. If what has been built survives, the builder will receive a reward. If it is burned up, the builder will suffer loss but yet will be saved – even though only as one escaping through the flames."[11]

Your personal salvation isn't the end – it's the beginning.

There is more to your current life. You know its true – you can feel it in your bones. You are being called into a great epic, and to play a role God has shaped just for you.

*The salvation that works in you,
is also designed to work through you.*

Ticket holders wait to go to heaven. Kingdom builders understand heaven is coming here – and seek to actively join the battle being waged against the forces of darkness that resist it. Ticket holders wallow in cursing the darkness. Kingdom builders delight in bringing light. Ticket holders think salvation is only about them personally. Kingdom builders understand that God is saving everything – its ripple effect starting with Christ, and expanding outward from those who are in Christ, and then eventually to all of creation.

---

10 | Scholar Dallas Willard called this "sin management." For an excellent exploration of this concept, see his book *The Divine Conspiracy*.

11 | 1 Corinthians 3:12-15

"Behold I make all things new."[12]

"...and through him to reconcile to himself all things, whether things on earth or things in heaven ..."[13]

"...the creation itself will be liberated from its bondage to decay and brought into the freedom and glory of the children of God."[14]

Divine Navy SEALS

You are being called into the greatest movement of liberation the world will ever know. The salvation of Jesus Christ is not merely something you receive by faith, but exercise by faith. The light of hope God has planted within you is meant to not just be comforting, but incendiary – a flame with spreads to others, a flame which passionately banishes the darkness from the world.

This lifestyle of active discipleship makes you an enemy of all forces opposed to the Kingdom of God. These were the same forces that Jesus aggressively went after during his ministry – sickness, pain, disability, demonic possession, poverty, condemnation, sin and death.

Seriously, did you ever really think about the miracles and acts of love Jesus performed while on earth? At first glance you might be tempted to think they were a waste of time – because they appeared to be temporary. The blind, the lame, the lepers, and even the dead people Jesus healed[15] all eventually died again. So what was the point?

This is where we must grasp the mystery of the Kingdom of God and the parables Jesus used to describe it – seed, yeast, wheat and weeds growing together, etc. Small, quiet and covert is the Kingdom. In Jesus, the rightful king has reappeared to reclaim that which is his – but not by brute and intimidating force, but rather through love and the exercise of free will. Think about it – what is love without free will?

---

12 | Revelation 21:5
13 | Colossians 1:20
14 | Romans 8 (read the whole chapter – it's pretty good!).
15 | This would be Lazarus (John 11), the son of the Widow of Nain (Luke 7), and Jairus' daughter (Matthew 9).

And this is our clue to the works of Jesus – they were not meant to be engagements of the final battle, but rather signs of the new reality breaking in to this fallen world – as if Jesus was saying "This is what things will be like when my Father is in control fully again."

Why just signs to start?

So that we would have the chance to join him in his counter-offensive once and for all of our own free will. So that our eyes might be opened once more to the true heart of God, choose love, and choose to fight for it.

In his book Mere Christianity, C.S. Lewis described it this way,

> "Why is God landing in this enemy-occupied world in disguise and starting a sort of secret society to undermine the devil? Why is He not landing in force, invading it? Is it that He is not strong enough? Well, Christians think He is going to land in force; we do not know when. But we can guess why He is delaying. He wants to give us the chance of joining His side freely.

> "I do not suppose you and I would have thought much of a Frenchman who waited till the Allies were marching into Germany and then announced he was on our side. God will invade. But I wonder whether people who ask God to interfere openly and directly in our world quite realise what it will be like when He does. When that happens, it is the end of the world. When the author walks on to the stage the play is over.

> "God is going to invade, all right: but what is the good of saying you are on His side then, when you see the whole natural universe melting away like a dream and something else – something it never entered your head to conceive – comes crashing in; something so beautiful to some of us and so terrible to others that none of us will have any choice left? For this time it will be God without disguise; something so overwhelming that it will strike either irresistible love or irresistible horror into every creature. It will be too late then to choose your side. There is no use saying you choose to lie down when it has become impossible to stand up.

"That will not be the time for choosing: it will be the time when we discover which side we really have chosen, whether we realised it before or not. Now, today, this moment, is our chance to choose the right side. God is holding back to give us that chance. It will not last forever. We must take it or leave it."

So often victory in military battles hinges not on the final assault, but rather the covert reconnaissance done before the main engagement. The work of behind-the-scenes special forces prepares the battlefield prior to the invasion. Today groups like the Navy SEALS are indispensable to victory – warriors who quietly invade hostile territory ahead of time and do the little, unnoticed things that will eventually make all the difference in the final battle. They are the quiet heroes.

To be a follower of Jesus in this moment of history is to choose to be a divine Navy SEAL. We embrace the quiet honor of occupying hostile territory and joining our king in representing the new, invading reality.

Our weapons are those of the spirit: Biblical truth, love, hope, forgiveness, sacrifice, prayer, patience, kindness, justice, freedom, perseverance in persecution and suffering, the Word of God, and of course, the Gospel itself.

This calling and high honor is not limited by age, gender, social status, geography, or any other false division promoted by this rebellious world. The gifting of the Holy Spirit is as diverse as there are people – and this is why the movement of Jesus is unstoppable. The work we do now, even when it may appear futile, is like seed. It is planted for the day when the Kingdom comes in its fullness. No act of love or work of justice done in the name of Jesus is ever wasted.

Samwise Gangee *(The Lord of the Rings)* was oh so right when in a deep moment of exhaustion and despair he reminded Frodo of this truth:

Sam: *It's like in the great stories, Mr. Frodo, the ones that really mattered. Full of darkness and danger they were, and sometimes you didn't want to know the end because how could the end be happy? How could the world go back to the way it was when so much bad had happened? But in the end,* *it's only a passing thing, this shadow, even darkness must pass. A new day will come, and when the sun shines, it'll shine out the clearer. Those were the stories that stayed with you, that meant something even if you were too small to understand why. But I think, Mr. Frodo, I do understand, I know now folk in those stories had lots of chances of turning back, only they didn't. They kept going because they were holding on to something.*

Frodo: *What are we holding onto, Sam?*

Sam: *That there's some good in the world, Mr. Frodo, and it's worth fighting for.*

"Just Burn It ..."

In my previous book, *The End is the Beginning*, I shared the story about a mission trip that our Bismarck, ND, youth group undertook to the inner city of Chicago.[16] Despite previous excursions elsewhere, Chicago proved to be a very eye-opening experience – not so much because of the poverty, but because of the role that deeply engrained sin played in the hopelessness of the area. Our group witnessed drug busts and heard gunshots on several evenings. We noticed that there was little fresh food in the grocery stores, and that thick Plexiglas barriers protected workers at fast food restaurants. We even washed blood off of walls and filled holes created by gunshots in the housing projects we were helping to renovate. On our first day of work, someone threw a two-by-four piece of wood through the back window of our bus. For safety considerations, we were advised to be in our living quarters by 4 p.m. because that was when what was called "The third shift" emerged – the gangs, dealers, and prostitutes.

Everyone did not universally welcome us – even among those we were trying to help.

It reminded us of what Jesus once said to those who would follow him,

---

16 | We were working in the Garfield Park district. It was the brutally hot summer of 1995.

"A servant is not greater than his master.' If they persecuted me, they will persecute you also."[17]

It was on this trip that many of us learned that the greatest expression of Christ-like love happens when it is given, but not reciprocated.

On our final day of ministry, our group was partnering with a local church in occupying a local park that was usually dominated by the local drug dealers and gangs. It was our second afternoon of doing this. Our weapons were a couple of snow cone stands, and our combined presence. The first afternoon, Chicago police cars circled our block every few minutes. The second afternoon, they added an armed officer.

Toward the end of the day, we struck up a conversation with the officer about the state of things in that part of Chicago. One of my colleagues, a youth director from Century Baptist Church in Bismarck,[18] asked the policeman what it would take to turn the neighborhood around for the long term. The officer was native to the city and we genuinely were curious as to his thoughts. I will never forget his words, or the vacant look on his face ...

"Just burn it. Burn it all down and start all over. There is no hope here. I appreciate what you all are trying to do here, but once you leave, it will just go back to the way things have always been here"

Sometimes it really does feel that way doesn't it? I remember the looks on the faces of our kids as we packed up and left that day. It was hard. There were a lot of tears. As the bus drove away, many of the children who dared to come out and play with us ran after the bus – as if they knew their moment in the sun was fading into the distance with our vehicle.

These can be heartbreaking moments if we choose to look at them through merely human eyes. But God reminds us to look at them differently – with his eyes.

---

17 | John 15:20
18 | Yes, believe it not, Lutherans and Baptists are fully capable of working together!

"Let us not become weary in doing good, for at the proper time we will reap a harvest if we do not give up."[19]

It would have been very easy for God to look upon the vast brokenness and evil of this world and say – Enough! Just burn it and start all over.

But he didn't, did he?

Instead he took our broken flesh upon himself and inaugurated the greatest invasion the world will ever know. He wants to save the world, not discard it – one heart at a time.

He wants to start with yours. And once he has yours, he wants you to covertly help him save others. It will be hard and there will be resistance, but it's a high honor to be asked to participate in rescuing the world.

Somewhere down in Hell there's a post office with wanted posters. Is your face on one of them?

Will you settle for just good behavior, or do you want to be dangerous?

---

19 | Galatians 6:9

Spiritual Gifts: Humility Or Hubris?

"When I was a boy of 14, my father was so ignorant I could hardly stand to have the old man around. But when I got to be 21, I was astonished at how much the old man had learned in seven years."

Mark Twain

One of the most popular TV shows over the past decade or so has been the singing talent show *American Idol*. To some degree, it is probably popular because it taps into the great American, "rags to riches," "little guy makes it big," story. People love to see the underdog overcome and achieve their dreams. This is why movies such as *Rocky* are so iconic in our culture. To a certain degree I think we all live vicariously through these people – connecting to their struggle while imagining what it would be like to live our dreams to the fullest.

However, for all the glory that is on full display for the winners during the final episodes of a given season, there is quite a bit of ugliness for the losers that are weeded out early at the start of the season. *American Idol*, unlike most talent shows, is not afraid to show this process and capitalize on the equally riveting drama of a train wreck.

Watching these early contestants is equally funny and painful. They think they are stars waiting to be discovered – but they are living in a dream world.

Singing? I'd rather listen to my fingernails run across a chalkboard.

Rhythm? It's like listening to someone fall down a long set of stairs.

Charisma? Well ... actually a lot of them have charisma – but it's a hyper, out of control type that I think they are mistaking for having actual talent.

The climax of many of these early auditions comes when the one judge in the group that actually has no problem being honest

(Simon Cowell) tells them the cold, hard truth – often in ways that are less than tactful. It is at this point that we get a real look into just how deeply a contestant has bought into the illusion that singing is their gift. Some will cry and whimper, and quietly leave the room. You feel bad for these people, but at least they are learning the truth, and to some degree, this may actually set them free to pursue their real gifts.

But then there are the contestants who refuse to accept the truth … These moments get ugly.

Maybe these people were told one too many times by their grandmas how "amazing" their voice is.

Maybe they read too many self-motivation books.

Maybe they bought into the uniquely American lie that, "you can do anything you dream if you just believe …" (I'm sorry folks – that is just not true and we would do well to raise our kids to align their dreams with how God made them, not their own egos).

Words are exchanged … often they are nasty ones. Men and women who have never earned a dollar singing presume to tell three music industry professionals with years of success and experience that they are wrong and wouldn't know talent if it came up and kicked them in the _ _ _ (three letter word, also a name for a donkey).

All you can do is just shake your head as you take in the spectacle.

I often wonder if that isn't how the Apostle Paul felt as he was writing his letters of encouragement to the young church in Corinth.

The Chaos in Corinth

Rather than becoming a cause of praise and celebration to God, the spiritual gifts in Corinth had become the epicenter of conflict. This was probably not a total surprise to Paul. The church in Corinth was an exciting, yet explosive mix of gentile and Jewish believers. Though their unity was in Christ, all of the groups brought competing worldviews, morals, religious and socio-economic assumptions into the practice of the church. Instead of submitting their past patterns of behavior to the new Christian ethic, these various groups were doing the opposite:

- Members were playing favorites with their leaders.[1]

- Sexual immorality was being tolerated within the ranks.[2]

- Lawsuits were brought between believers, stifling their witness.[3]

- Worship was a mess because believing women who hailed as priestesses from prior pagan religions needed to submit to a more humble and conservative code for the sake of order.[4]

- Wealthy believers were distorting the practice of communion (commonly referred to then as the "Love Feast," because the ceremony was often embedded into an actual meal).[5]

Nowhere was this volatility more pronounced than in the practice of the spiritual gifts. That which was supposed to bind the Corinthian church together was tearing it apart. A false hierarchy of spiritual gifting had developed that was dishonoring to God. Put simply, the members of this community were committing two fundamental mistakes; one group thought too much of their spiritual gifting while the other group thought too little of their spiritual gifting. One group was like Narcissus, the other like Icarus. Both serve as cautionary figures about the danger of pride. Who are Narcissus and Icarus? Well … let's read on.

Spiritual Gifts: The Narcissus Mistake

Narcissus was the son of the river god Cephissus and the nymph Leiriope. He was an extremely good-looking Greek youth. His beauty ultimately led to his death. Narcissus was so handsome that many women and men fell in love with him. He rejected all of them. Ameinias was so devastated by Narcissus' indifference toward him that he killed himself. Before doing so, however, Ameinias called on the gods to punish Narcissus.

---

1 | 1 Corinthians 1:10-12
2 | 1 Corinthians 5
3 | 1 Corinthians 6
4 | 1 Corinthians 11
5 | 1 Corinthians 11

They caused the beautiful youth to gaze into a pond at his reflection. He fell in love with his own image and drowned trying to touch it.[6]

There were some in the Corinthian church who thought too much of their spiritual gifts. Like Narcissus, they loved their own spirituality to the scorn of others. They failed to understand that their gifting was to be exercised in loving service for God's glory – not put on display for their own glory. Paul cleverly uses the metaphor of the human body to underscore the equal importance of all gifted members.

> *"The eye cannot say to the hand, 'I don't need you!' And the head cannot say to the feet, 'I don't need you!' On the contrary, those parts of the body that seem to be weaker are indispensable, and the parts that we think are less honorable we treat with special honor. And the parts that are unpresentable are treated with special modesty, while our presentable parts need no special treatment.*

> *"But God has put the body together, giving greater honor to the parts that lacked it, so that there should be no division in the body, but that its parts should have equal concern for each other. If one part suffers, every part suffers with it; if one part is honored, every part rejoices with it. Now you are the body of Christ, and each one of you is a part of it."[7]*

"If one part suffers, every part suffers with it ..."

My sophomore year of college I learned the literal meaning of Paul's metaphor. I was a scholarship basketball player at Bismarck State College on a team that had the talent and aspirations to go deep into the national junior college playoffs. There was just one problem – my left big toe was starting to hurt like crazy. An X-ray from the team doctor revealed the cause – a hairline fracture. I had been playing with a broken big toe. Worse yet, it was my left big toe. Why was that such a big deal? I was right-handed, and for right-handed players, the left leg is the power leg – the leg that you jump off of most often. And, as I discovered, it was extremely painful to jump off of that leg if your big toe was broken. Though seemingly small and insignificant, though almost always hidden

---

6 | Read more at mythencyclopedia.com
7 | 1 Corinthians 12:21-27

from view, that big toe was indispensable to my ability to function as a basketball player.

So it is with the body of Christ. Everybody matters. But some lost sight of that in the ripples of their own reflection.

Those who had the supernatural gift of speaking in tongues seemed to be the primary instigators of this issue and the people most in need of correction.[8] Paul aggressively reminds these people that not only are all of the spiritual gifts important, but that some of the gifts actually exceeded tongues in importance.

> "Anyone who speaks in a tongue edifies themselves, but the one who prophesies edifies the church. I would like every one of you to speak in tongues, but I would rather have you prophesy. The one who prophesies is greater than the one who speaks in tongues, unless someone interprets, so that the church may be edified.

> "Now, brothers and sisters, if I come to you and speak in tongues, what good will I be to you, unless I bring you some revelation or knowledge or prophecy or word of instruction? ...

> "So it is with you. **Since you are eager for gifts of the Spirit, try to excel in those that build up the church."**

And so Paul sought to right the ship from a bunch of people who were looking over the side at their own reflections. But there was a second group that also needed attending to as well. This group didn't think they were all that important, and depending upon how they reacted to that misperception, could also be a problem if not corrected and encouraged.

Spiritual Gifts: The Icarus Mistake

In Greek mythology, **Icarus** is the son of the master craftsman Daedalus, the creator of the Labyrinth. Often depicted in art,

---

8 | It is an unfortunate truth that this problem still exists in the body of Christ today. Some groups of Pentecostal believers still teach that speaking in tongues is the primary evidence of one being a true believer in Christ.

Icarus and his father attempt to escape from Crete by means of wings that his father constructed from feathers and wax. Icarus' father warns him first of complacency and then of hubris (pride), asking that he fly neither too low nor too high, so the sea's dampness would not clog his wings or the sun's heat melt them. Icarus ignored his father's instructions not to fly too close to the sun, whereupon the wax in his wings melted and he fell into the sea.[9]

Now when referring to people within the Corinthian church who felt that their gifts were unimportant you might be asking, "how can these people be accused of pride?" That's a fair question, and it certainly is not my intention to unfairly criticize people who feel insignificant. But such people have more in common with Icarus than you might think. Remember, Icarus had to navigate between two equally dangerous routes – descending too low, and reaching too high.

Metaphorically speaking, descending too low is the act of becoming irrelevant by yielding to despair. This group believes they do not have anything of worth to offer, and thus reflects this with their behavior – they do nothing. In short – they fly too close to the sea.

Conversely, reaching too high is the act of becoming irrelevant by aspiring beyond your calling and giftedness. This group seeks to overcompensate – stifling their actual gifting in a bad trade in order to satisfy the hunger of their ego. In short – they fly too close to the sun.

A good example of the "reaching too high" group is, interestingly enough, the 18th President of the United States, Ulysses S. Grant. John Ortberg writes about the paradox of a man who, though immensely gifted, still flew too close to the sun.

> "William McFeely's biography of Ulysses Grant describes a man who was masterfully fitted for military leadership and writing (his Memoirs are considered a classic of military literature) but horribly ill-equipped for business and politics. Grant neither understood nor enjoyed life in Washington, and he is usually judged to have been one of the least effective presidents of the United States. In his final – and extraordinary – State of

---

9 | Taken from Wikipedia

the Union message, he apologized for his ineptness: "It was my fortune, or misfortune, to be called to the office of Chief Executive without any previous political training."

"Why, then, did this Civil War hero work so hard for a job he neither enjoyed nor understood? "His personal need was to retain the immense respect in which he was held everywhere in the North. . . He wanted to matter in a world he had been watching closely all his life. A little recognition – a little understanding that he did know what he was doing – was all he required. He needed to be taken into account." **His own unmet needs for acceptance and wholeness blinded him to acknowledging his limitations."[10]**

Don't reach too high … don't descend too low.

Paul encourages the Icarus group with a gentle and encouraging reminder that know matter what the appearances, their gifting matters, and they are exactly where God wants them.

"Just as a body, though one, has many parts, but all its many parts form one body, so it is with Christ. For we were all baptized by one Spirit so as to form one body – whether Jews or Gentiles, slave or free – and we were all given the one Spirit to drink. Even so the body is not made up of one part but of many.

"Now if the foot should say, "Because I am not a hand, I do not belong to the body," it would not for that reason stop being part of the body. And if the ear should say, "Because I am not an eye, I do not belong to the body," it would not for that reason stop being part of the body. If the whole body were an eye, where would the sense of hearing be? If the whole body were an ear, where would the sense of smell be? But in fact God has placed the parts in the body, every one of them, just as he wanted them to be. If they were all one part, where would the body be?"

The Use and Misuse of Gifts

Spiritual gifts, though given by God, are instrumental in nature. In other words, though designed for good, they can be used in not so good ways.

10 | Excerpt From: John Ortberg. "If You Want to Walk on Water, You've Got to Get Out of the Boat."

I learned this reality at a very early age.

I am the oldest of three brothers. I love Bob (middle) and Mike (youngest) and appreciate them. I am thrilled that even though I am the oldest, at this stage of our lives, I have the most hair. Anyway ...

Somewhere around the age of 7, before my youngest brother Mike was born, Bob and I spent our summer days with a baby-sitter out on a farm east of our hometown of Rugby, ND. It was a glorious place for two young boys to enjoy the outdoors, and we exhausted ourselves daily with all kinds of rural adventures.

One day we were walking alongside the cow pasture when I made the mistake of attempting to join the cattle by swinging under the fence ... the electric fence. Now, let me explain. We have an electric fence today out at our ranch, but it is for horses. Horses are far more sensitive than cattle, so the voltage needed to control them is far less. The fence I swung under was not for horses. Remember ... it was for cattle.

I might have screamed...
There might have been the faint smell of smoke wafting in the air.

Bob thought it was hilarious. He laughed so hard he peed his pants (which at his age didn't take much). You know that phrase "There is no fury like a woman scorned"? Well just think of the seven-year-old version of that and you will understand my state of mind. No five-year-old could laugh at me and get away with it ...

Having experienced first-hand the wonders of electricity, I decided to learn more about it. This is where I had a distinct advantage over Bob at that time – I had the gift of literacy (somewhat) and he did not. In addition, my parents had also bought these books for us – Childcraft Encyclopedias. I immersed myself in the world of Edison and Tesla as I plotted my pre-school revenge.

I read and read. And then ... EUREKA! I found it. That one scrap of information that would help me get even with my smart-aleck sibling; wood was a very poor conductor of electricity. This was going to be easier than I had even dreamed ...

One lazy summer morning, a few weeks after the psychological trauma had subsided, Bob and I found ourselves walking by the very same spot next to the cattle pasture. Pointing to the fence I casually, yet deviously, suggested that Bob swing under it into the pasture.

"No way … I saw what happened to you, I don't want to get a big shock!" Exclaimed Bob.

"It's OK," I said, "they turned off the fence. It isn't even on."

"Yea right … I don't believe you. Liar, liar pants on fire."

(He was right, of course, I was lying. But it wasn't my pants that were about to be on fire.)

"No really, I'm not lying," I assured him, "Watch, I'll prove it to you."

As I picked up the small wooden stick lying on the ground, I couldn't help but contemplate in my tiny child-like way the saying, "Knowledge is power." Knowledge really is power. It was a gift. A gift that I was about to grievously misuse.

"See," I said, uneventfully touching the stick to the hotwire, "I told you, it's off."

I couldn't believe how easily he fell for it. Even today, I have faint memories of a crackling sound, screaming, cries of betrayal, and being carried off to the farmhouse by our babysitter for the spanking of my life.[11] I might have squeezed out a vengeful smile or two between swats.

I had gained the ability to read. I had been resourced by my parents with the Childcraft Encyclopedias. I had the knowledge, and it was powerful.

I had the gifts, but I didn't have the love.

---

11 | Don't freak out. This was a very common punishment in my day.

"And Yet I Will Show You the Most Excellent Way ..."

For Paul, the most important aspect of spiritual gifting didn't start with the gift itself, but rather the extent one's heart was submitted to the giver of the gift.

In the battle for the Kingdom of God, though the spiritual gift is the weapon, humility is the targeting system.

The most powerful spiritual gifts always start with a heart submitted to God. In this way, all spiritual gifts are to be shaped by the ultimate spiritual gift – Christ-like love.

The Greek word for this love is Agape.

This is the love always associated with God Himself. It is a love utterly unattainable by human effort. You can only practice Agape by letting God love others through you. It specializes in humility, sacrifice, mercy, forgiveness, and perseverance. This is the most potent gift. This is the most powerful weapon. Submitting your gifts and very identity to this love constitutes Paul's prescription for the dysfunctional believers in Corinth.

> "Are all apostles? Are all prophets? Are all teachers? Do all work miracles? Do all have gifts of healing? Do all speak in tongues? Do all interpret? Now eagerly desire the greater gifts. And yet I will show you the most excellent way.

> "If I speak in the tongues of men or of angels, but do not have love, I am only a resounding gong or a clanging cymbal. If I have the gift of prophecy and can fathom all mysteries and all knowledge, and if I have a faith that can move mountains, but do not have love, I am nothing. If I give all I possess to the poor and give over my body to hardship that I may boast, but do not have love, I gain nothing.

> "Love is patient, love is kind. It does not envy, it does not boast, it is not proud. It does not dishonor others, it is not self-seeking, it

is not easily angered, it keeps no record of wrongs. Love does not delight in evil but rejoices with the truth. It always protects, always trusts, always hopes, always perseveres.

"Love never fails. But where there are prophecies, they will cease; where there are tongues, they will be stilled; where there is knowledge, it will pass away. For we know in part and we prophesy in part, but when completeness comes, what is in part disappears. When I was a child, I talked like a child, I thought like a child, I reasoned like a child. When I became a man, I put the ways of childhood behind me. For now we see only a reflection as in a mirror; then we shall see face to face. Now I know in part; then I shall know fully, even as I am fully known.

"And now these three remain: faith, hope and love. But the greatest of these is love."

I do about ten weddings every year, and you can bet that these verses from 1 Corinthians 13 show up in most of them. And yet the love Paul is describing here makes any form of romantic love superficial by comparison. But maybe that's the point – in a real marriage, it is going to take far more than romance to keep you strong. It is going to take the love of Christ himself, and the only way to love like that is to humbly submit to it and let it flow through you.

Paul stresses that all spiritual gifts are rendered impotent without love, and that eventually none of these gifts will remain except for love. It is simultaneously a sobering and liberating thought – start with love, and you will get the gifts thrown in. But pridefully focus on the gifts only, and eventually there will be no "you" left to go on after everything has faded from existence except love.

Again view it as if humble love is the targeting system. How potent can a spiritual gift be if it is patient and kind? How powerful can a spiritual gift be if it is not envious, boastful, dishonoring or self-seeking? How liberating can a spiritual gift be if it always protects, trusts, hopes and perseveres?

You get my point.

Hubris or humility? When it comes to the spiritual gifts, the choice is yours, although I think it is obvious.

Don't be like Narcissus and fall in love with your own reflection.

Don't mimic Icarus and fly too close to the sea, or too near the sun.

Reject the illusion and temptation of being a spiritual American Idol, but instead choose to love the Giver even more than the gift.

Paul is right ... it is the most excellent way.

Spiritual Gifts: Do You Make The List?

"Don't ask what the world needs. Ask what makes you come alive, and go do it. Because what the world needs is people who have come alive."

Howard Thurman, Author of *Jesus and the Disinherited*

In 1980 I was on an awesome football team. I was in eighth grade, attending Simle Jr. High in Bismarck, ND. We didn't lose a game that year, going 8-0. In fact, we didn't even give up a score until the final game of the year when one of our defensive backs committed the cardinal sin of letting a receiver get behind him – giving up a late touchdown pass.

I won't get into whom the defensive back was ...[1]

One of the reasons we were so good was that we were blessed with talented players who could play multiple positions depending upon what was needed to win in any given game. Our coaches weren't shy about shuffling us around if it might give us an advantage. Believe it or not, I was one of those players – not because I was speedy (erosion might be faster than me) or strong (unless body odor counted) ... no I was interchangeable because I could throw the ball ... a ... really ... long ... ways.

So, whenever our coaches felt like scoring a quick touchdown ,they would just have me and the quarterback switch positions. His name was Chuck and he was the biggest and strongest player on the team. I don't remember the technical name for the play, but it always amounted to something like, "Chuck go deep and Randy throw the ball as far as you can." As best as I can remember it worked every time. Even though I wasn't the quarterback, I probably threw about seven or eight touchdown passes that season.

---

1 | Confidentiality prevents me from revealing his identity but his initials were Randy Upgren. ☺

There was just one catch ... I never saw a single one of them.

Deep passes require time to develop. Every time I dropped back to pass, I had to wait as long as possible for Chuck to get down the field. The sequence of events inevitably always went something like this:

"Hike"

Drop back (count "1 ...2 ... 3 ...")

Close eyes ...

Throw the ball as far as I can ...

Just as ball leaves hand, get absolutely CRUSHED by defensive lineman ...

See big star, which then fades away ... find myself looking up at the sky ...

Hear the crowd cheer wildly ... (indicating that Chuck caught the ball and then proceeded to run over remaining tiny defenders on his way into the end zone ...)

I'm not sure how "glorious" football felt, lying there on the ground as all my teammates ran to the end zone to celebrate with Chuck ..."[2]

When it comes to spiritual gifts, I wonder how many Christians are actually throwing touchdowns but never see them ... or are appreciated for them.

Misunderstanding Paul's Lists: Limits or Possibilities?

One of my pet peeves about how spiritual gifting is often taught and understood in the church involves the way the biblical verses are approached. Often taken out of context, these verses treat

---

2 | In all fairness Chuck was a good teammate, and always credited me with good passes – as painful as they might have been.

Paul's words as if he is providing an exhaustive list of the spiritual gifts, and that if you are a mature Christian you will find yourself somewhere on the list.

AAARRRGGGGHHHHH !!! Do you know why this drives me crazy?

It is because this way of reading the scriptures has a way of marginalizing and discouraging so many sincere disciples of Jesus. As a pastor in the church for the last twenty-five years, I can't tell you how many times I have heard good and gifted believers express their sense of inadequacy based upon these texts:

"I don't think I'm good at anything on Paul's lists ..."

"I just feel so average when I read about the spiritual gifts ..."

"If the church is a body, then I feel like the fuzz that collects in the belly-button ..."

Most books and assessment on the topic don't help. Too often they act as if Paul is giving an exhaustive list, and then impose analysis on readers that pigeonhole them between the boundaries of the list.

For example, below are the two major lists Paul writes of in his letters to Rome and Corinth.

> *"We have different gifts, according to the grace given to each of us. If your gift is prophesying, then prophesy in accordance with your faith; if it is serving, then serve; if it is teaching, then teach; if it is to encourage, then give encouragement; if it is giving, then give generously; if it is to lead, do it diligently; if it is to show mercy, do it cheerfully.*[3]

> *"Now you are the body of Christ, and each one of you is a part of it. And God has placed in the church first of all apostles, second prophets, third teachers, then miracles, then gifts of healing, of helping, of guidance, and of different kinds of tongues."*[4]

---

3 | Romans 12
4 | 1 Corinthians 12

Never mind that different circumstances in Rome and Corinth were motivating each letter. Never mind that the gifts Paul lists don't even constitute the main point Paul is trying to get across. If we choose to yank his words out of context we can come up with this nice, neat list that all good, mature Christians should fit into:

Gifts:
1. Serving
2. Teaching
3. Encouraging
4. Giving
5. Leading
6. Acts of mercy
7. Prophecy[5]
8. Works of miracles
9. Healing
10. Helping
11. Guidance or discernment
12. Diverse tongues

The problem isn't the various gifts listed. The problem is what we do with them. We damage Paul's intent in two ways: We *quantify* them, and then we (for lack of a better word) *churchify* them. Both are limitations. One is an artificial limitation of quantity, the other of quality.

Here is what I mean ...

The Fallacy of Quantifying the Gifts

Paul lists twelve spiritual gifts in his two letters. But let's think about this objectively and biblically – do you really think **all** of the spiritual gifts are listed?

What about music?[6] Music has been present within the structure of worship in nearly all religions since the beginning of recorded history. This is especially true of the Jewish and Christian faiths (I seem to recall a book in the Old Testament called the Psalms

---

5 | Paul would later also list evangelism as a gift in reference to his understudy Timothy.

6 | Let's also not forget the other fine arts. Would anyone deny the spiritual giftedness of Leonardo Da Vinci or Michelangelo?

which were a collection of Jewish hymns). King David had the gift of music and used it to soothe King Saul's anxieties.[7] Peter took great encouragement from music while in prison,[8] and Paul encouraged the saints to lift each other up with "psalms, hymns and spiritual songs."[9] Later in history Martin Luther would say that apart from the Word of God, music was the greatest gift of God.

What about the gift of learning or study? This is not teaching in the strictest sense of passing down already established knowledge, but instead conveys the idea of exploring and discovering new knowledge. Nothing is mentioned in the words of Paul, or for that matter, the New Testament about the edification that scholarship can bring to people's sense of knowledge, awe, wonder and worship of God. The Old Testament praises those who seek to explore the mysteries of God and his creation.

Psalm 111:2
"Great are the works of the Lord, studied by all who delight in them."

Daniel 1:17
"As for these four youths, God gave them learning and skill in all literature and wisdom, and Daniel had understanding in all visions and dreams ..."

Can anyone doubt that the world was blessed immensely by the scholarly work of Christians such as Galileo, Isaac Newton, Johannes Keppler or Francis Collins?[10] To think that Spirit-led scholarship isn't a spiritual gift seems needlessly rigid to me![11]

And finally ... what about justice? The Hebrew word *mishpot* is the Old Testament word for justice, and is one of the most thematically

---

7 | 1 Samuel 16:23
8 | Acts 16:25
9 | Ephesians 5:18, Colossians 3:16
10 | Don't recognize the name Francis Collins? He is a Christian scientist who was the first head of the modern Human Genome Project. See his book *The Language of God* for his amazing story.
11 | By the way ... don't fall for the modern-day fallacy that science and the Christian faith have historically been bitter enemies. Nothing could be further from the truth. For excellent reading on this subject, see Rodney Stark's *The Triumph of Christianity* and James Sire's *The Universe Next Door*.

emphasized words in the Bible. Over and over, the Old Testament prophets called out for justice to be done among God's people as a sign of their covenant faithfulness:

Amos 5:24
"But let justice roll on like a river, righteousness like a never-failing stream!"

Psalm 37:28
"For the LORD loves the just and will not forsake his faithful ones."

Micah 6:8
"He has shown you, O mortal, what is good. And what does the LORD require of you? To act justly and to love mercy and to walk humbly with your God."

The New Testament also rings with the importance of justice in the life of any faithful follower of God. Jesus echoes the prophets when he says,

Matthew 23:23
"Woe to you, teachers of the law and Pharisees, you hypocrites! You give a tenth of your spices—mint, dill and cumin. But you have neglected the more important matters of the law—justice, mercy and faithfulness. You should have practiced the latter, without neglecting the former."

All of this and yet Paul doesn't list this among the spiritual gifts. Are we suggesting that those who fight for justice in the world aren't spiritually gifted? I hope not! The world needs more Harriet Tubmans, Nelson Mandelas, and Martin Luther Kings.

And so, we find three pretty significant examples of biblically and historically acknowledged spiritual gifts that are not listed by Paul or the New Testament.[12] Does this mean we shouldn't trust the texts? Of course not. What it means is that we should understand that Paul's lists represent broad examples and possibilities, not

---

12| Hospitality is another spiritual gift I think is significant and has been written about extensively by Henry Nouwen. As someone of Lutheran heritage, it would be blasphemy to disregard as unspiritual the tradition of a good potluck dinner. And what about Esther? What spiritual gift did she exercise in saving the Hebrews from Haman's genocidal plot? Funny – I don't see "super-hot babe" listed among Paul's spiritual gifts!

categories. Indeed, I would assert that the spiritual gifts are as diverse as there are people, as creative as there is vision and ideas.

The Fallacy of "Churchifying" the Gifts

I put the word "churchifying" in quotes because clearly I have coined a word to describe a concept. The concept involves the idea that we have a tendency to limit where and how spiritual gifts are used by the church and its vocations. So ... I think the word is correct – "churchify."

But doesn't Paul say that the spiritual gifts are for the edification of the church?[13] Yes ... But that is not a function of geopgraphy, it is a function of mission. Jesus gives the church its most important and defining command in Matthew 28 when he says, *"Go and make disciples of all nations, baptizing in the name of the Father, Son and Holy Spirit, and teaching them to obey everything I have commanded you."* The purpose of the spiritual gifts is to empower the great commission in the world, while shaping the hearts of people within the church.

However, we just seem to have this tendency to conform the exercise of spiritual giftedness within the walls of the church building. As a result, the same list Paul offers often gets distorted, defined and expressed in ways such as this (WARNING: The following is extremely sarcastic):

1. Serving (Make weak coffee for fellowship between services)

2. Teaching (Who wouldn't want to volunteer in Sunday School to tell little in Billy about Jesus while trying to prevent him from eating glue?)

3. Encouraging (Write some nice notes to the staff while slipping in a passive aggressive comment about how the church may need to up its insurance in case the youth pastor sets the building on fire)

---

13 | 1 Corinthians 14:12

4. Giving (Tithing is a spiritual gift for rich doctors, the rest of us can just give 2 percent – as long we are joyful about it)

5. Leading (Pastor, as president of this council for the last 33 years, I'm here to remind you just who pays your salary ...)

6. Acts of mercy (Visiting the sick? That's the pastor's job)

7. Prophecy (A position and gift that is self-appointed, gives license to occasionally publically advocate personal issues and agendas in the name of the LORD)

8. Works of miracles (Lord, restore this nation back to the way it was in the perfect days of 1950)

9. Healing (We could visit the AIDS ward at the hospital but we would rather pray one more time for Irma's bunions)

10. Helping (The Associate Pastor is in the nursery changing diapers and needs help? Sorry – not my spiritual gift ... besides, it's Easter!)

11. Guidance or discernment (What? We need more staff? Just get more volunteers)

12. Diverse tongues (Not even going to touch that one)

Ok, you got me – I'm busted. Guilty as charged of gross exaggeration and attempting to use blatant stereotypes and humor to provoke deeper thought.

But ... my point still stands. We have a tendency to limit spiritual gifts and calling to within the confines of the church and the vocation of the pastor.

Biblically, the spiritual gifts should be exercised in two directions – outwardly to the world for the purpose of the Great Commission, and inwardly for the health of the community of faith. In this sense, I am really quite proud of my church, Charity Lutheran, because you can find many examples of this vibrant, bi-directional giftedness. Consider some of the examples from Paul's list one more time in light of the ministries of the people of Charity Lutheran Church:

Serving

Inward: Funeral Hospitality Team
Outward: Care Company Fix it Team

Encouragement

Inward: Stephen Ministry
Outward: Providence Ranch Youth Mentoring

Acts of Mercy

Inward: Church Crisis Fund
Outward: Kover's for Kids Blanket Ministry

Healing

Inward: Charity Prayer Team
Outward: One More One Less Orphan Adoption

Teaching

Inward: Life-Long Learning Group
Outward: WOW Outreach Worship

Other ministries of note at Charity that nurture and employ the giftedness of its disciples include Strongman men's ministries, Freedom Fellowship Outreach Church (Native American reservation), and the Dream Team worship and tech support team.

Examples such as these illustrate the expansive and creative expression of the spiritual gifts in the New Testament. Paul's list doesn't close the door, but rather opens the door to the calling of all people in all its diversity and possibilities. This was the energy behind the doctrine that Martin Luther would later call, "the priesthood of all believers."

The Big Takeaway and the Story of William Wilberforce

So what's the big takeaway? Well, its twofold:

1. Paul's words regarding spiritual gifts in scripture are meant to guide and encourage us, not constrain and discourage us.

They provide a starting point, not a wall. The only boundary Paul stresses is that our gifts, passions, talents, resources, and experiences be shaped by love and exercised in the name of Jesus.

2. Spiritual giftedness and calling is not limited to use in the church, or within the vocation of the pastor. Rather, the spiritual gifts are to be shaped by the Great Commission and explosively let loose in all directions. God's calling comes to all people. One can seek out spiritual giftedness and service just as easily on the sports field, in the workplace, or within the classroom as in the church itself.

C.S. Lewis once remarked about Christian vocation,

> *"The application of Christian principles, say, to trade unionism or education, must come from Christian trade unionists and Christian schoolmasters: just as Christian literature comes from Christian novelists and dramatists – not from the bench of bishops getting together and trying to write plays and novels in their spare time."*

William Wilberforce was a human force of nature. Within his lifetime (1759-1833) as a member of Parliament, he was instrumental in the establishment of prison reforms, animal cruelty laws, child labor protections, and of course, the abolition of slavery in England. Wilberforce at one point supported 69 charitable organizations, and is reported to have regularly given twenty-five percent of his income toward causes he saw as consistent with the Kingdom of God.

And yet, it almost didn't happen …

Early in his life, young William was brought up in the myopic world of wealth and social privilege. Gifted with people skills, Wilberforce was quite popular in college with his colleagues, and his socializing often led to less than stellar efforts in the classroom. Nonetheless, he was elected to Parliament at a young age where he spent the first years in a self-confessed state of narcissism,

> *"The first years in Parliament I did nothing – nothing to any purpose. My own distinction was my darling object."*

Though naturally gifted in many ways, William Wilberforce's own immature character squandered their impact. That is, until Easter morning of 1786 when he experienced a spiritual rebirth in Jesus Christ. So profound was the shift that William actually considered abandoning his political career for the clergy, thinking this was the proper place for his new world view. Thankfully his good friend William Pitt, who went on to become Prime Minister, convinced him otherwise. In a letter to his dear friend, Pitt wrote:

"Surely the principles as well as the practice of Christianity are simple and lead not to meditation only, but to action."

And indeed, for Wilberforce, Christian faith meant action. He could not stand idly by and see the image of God in each person blatantly abused for profit. His fiercely unpopular crusade against the slave trade ravaged his health and cost him politically. He endured verbal assaults and was even challenged to a duel by an angry slave-ship captain.

Even so, Wilberforce persevered year after year. Writing about whether to give up the fight, Wilberforce notes, "a man who fears God is not at liberty" to do so.

And so, William Wilberforce changed the world. Not because he became a clergyman, and not because he limited his work to within the church. He changed the world because he brought to bear who he was; his intellect, relationships, resources, and natural gifts, under the lordship of Jesus Christ. The rest, you might say, is history.

Believe it or not, God made you like William; with a specific shape and for a specific time to make a difference to specific persons.

You were designed to throw touchdowns ... don't doubt it for a second.

Adversity:
God's Growth Hormone

"And once the storm is over, you won't remember how you made it through, how you managed to survive. You won't even be sure, whether the storm is really over. But one thing is certain. When you come out of the storm, you won't be the same person who walked in. That's what the storm is all about."

Haruki Murakami

Last night, as I was channel surfing before going to bed, I came across an infomercial for the latest fitness program. It was called Body Beast. Normally I would just move on but this one hooked me because they had a 57-year-old man giving testimony about how this program had "changed his life." It was a little surreal watching him – like looking at a bad Photoshop of an old man's head attached to a twenty-year-old body.

"Wow," I thought, "is that real?"

Then they showed the 'before and after' photos. That was a little disheartening. His "after" body was, of course, amazing. But his 57-year-old "before" body was far better than my 49-year-old body. In fact I think it was better than my 21-year-old body.

That's when the infomercial lost me. But it hooks more than enough people doesn't it? Below is a sampling of the fitness crazes I have bought into:

- Total Gym (Chuck Norris convinced me – at least it didn't take up too much space)
- Soloflex (way back in the day – it made a good clothes rack)
- Tony Little's work out videos (I'm embarrassed by this one)
- Cross Fit (loved it – got me in the best shape of my adult life – until I ripped my knee to shreds)

So here is the dirty little secret about all of them: THEY WORK.

That's right – if you do them consistently, they all work. The machines or methods aren't the issue. It's the price that is the issue. No, I'm not talking about the cost of the programs or machines themselves. I'm talking about the price it takes to actually get in shape. It involves sweat, soreness, discipline and self-denial. This is why the fitness industry is so successful at reinventing itself – because every new craze lures people into thinking, *"this is the one – this is method where I can get the results without paying the price."*

And so we flutter about like butterflies, floating from one craze to another. We bang the drums, throw medicine balls at walls, spin till we drop, and Zumba our butts into oblivion. Don't get me wrong – I value exercise and think it's important. I just think we tend to always be open to a shortcut.

But there are no shortcuts.[1]

There's a reason you will never see an Olympic athlete sign an endorsement deal with Barcalounger recliners.

The general rule of exercise is pretty simple: Resistance makes you stronger.

When you exercise you are introducing controlled resistance into your body movements. This resistance pushes your body to the point of its limits, forcing it to rebuild itself during periods of rest.[2] Great trainers understand just how far to push a person, and also vary the kinds of resistance so that the body cannot adjust and compensate in ways that stifle growth.

What is true for the body can be even truer for the soul.

Adversity is God's growth hormone. He is the greatest trainer of all.

By and large, most people deeply desire to know God's will for their lives.

---

1 | I take that back. There are some shortcuts – but none without a steep price. (i.e., steroids).

2 | Of course this basic rule manifests itself differently for people of different ages.

By and large, most people deeply desire to discover their spiritual gifting.

By and large, most people deeply desire to be difference makers.

But unfortunately ... by and large, most people also would rather avoid the resistance and pain that comes with all of that.

By and large ... most people want the gain without the pain. They want the gift without the character training. Put simply, they want the shortcut.

Be honest ... do you ever wish there was a shortcut? Its OK – growth starts with acknowledging reality. Besides, you're in good company. Plenty of our Bible "heroes" wished for the same thing.

The Paradox of "Arriving"

In American culture the word "arrive" has become associated with reaching the summit of success. When an athlete wins a championship, or a lawyer makes "partner" in the firm, or an actor wins an Oscar, we like to say that they have "arrived." To "arrive" means you are reaping the reward of paying the price of success. In America "arriving" generally signifies the end of training. With God it often signals the beginning ...

- In Genesis 25, Jacob cons a hungry Esau out his birthright, as well as deceiving his father into giving him the blessing that is due Esau. Jacob, by hook and crook, has managed to "arrive" – but it is only the beginning of a life on the run in which God will quite literally wrestle him into submission, ultimately shaping him to become the namesake of a nation (Israel).

- In Genesis 37, Joseph receives dreams from the LORD that suggest he has a big future; a future that includes the audacious vision of his father and brothers bowing down to him. In Joseph's mind he has "arrived," but little does he realize that he has 20 years of heartbreaking training ahead of him before he will be worthy to inherit the vision God has given him.

- In Judges 13, Samson has called upon the LORD to protect Israel from its enemies. The LORD gifts Samson with unmatched strength. A Nazarite consecrated to the LORD, Samson thinks he has arrived and takes for granted his strength. But as strong as Samson's body is, his heart is still in need of training and humility. This period will prepare Samson to pay the ultimate price on behalf of his people.

- 1 Samuel 16, tells of a wonder-kid name David. David is a man who seeks after God's own heart. Due to King Saul's disobedience to the LORD, the prophet Samuel anoints David king at a young age. It appears David has arrived and his path is laid out before him. But unbeknownst to David the path would involve years of exile, adversity, rejection and heartbreak before his anointing is consummated with the crown.

- In the Book of Esther, we read of a beautiful young woman named Hadassah. Born into exile under the Persian king Xerxes, Hadassah is recruited into harem of women from which a replacement will be chosen to replace the deposed queen, Vashti. Hadassah is blessed by the LORD with beauty that surpasses all others, and she is made queen of Persia, assuming the new name Esther. In all worldly respects Esther has arrived. But she would soon realize that her position would serve a much greater purpose – a purpose that pushes her to new levels of courage and risk.

- The prophet Elijah has just won a stunning, supernatural victory over the prophets of Baal at Mount Carmel (1 Kings 18). Displaying stunning faith and courage, Elijah resists the false Gods promoted by the evil queen Jezebel. It constitutes a career defining moment. But even as it appears Elijah has "arrived", his life is threatened and he runs and hides in the mountains, enduring a period of deep despair and isolation. Even for a renowned prophet of God, there is still much to learn.

Do you see the pattern yet? (It's kind of unavoidable, isn't it?)

Don't, however, think this pattern of arrival and then training is limited to the characters of scripture.

Former U.S. President Teddy Roosevelt understood this truth and embraced it throughout his lifetime. Born a sickly child, young Teddy struggled mightily with asthma and debilitating congestion that hindered his ability to participate in the normal activities young boys enjoyed. It is said that in order to combat it, his father would take him on long horseback rides at night – the cool air and the rhythmic gate of the horse loosening his congestion and giving him relief.

Not content to live a life of limitation, the growing Teddy pro-actively embraced what he called *the strenuous life*.[3] He integrated his exuberant personality, vast range of interests, and world-famous achievements into a "cowboy" persona defined by robust masculinity.

However, the young Roosevelt would learn that although sometimes we choose *the strenuous life*, there are other times the strenuous life chooses us. It is in those moments we are tested to our very core.

On his 22nd birthday, Roosevelt married socialite Alice Hathaway Lee. Their daughter, Alice Lee Roosevelt, was born on February 12, 1884. Roosevelt's wife died two days after giving birth due to an undiagnosed case of kidney failure, which had been undetected due to the pregnancy.

In his diary entry for that dark day, Roosevelt wrote a large 'X' on the page and followed by, *"The light has gone out of my life."* His mother, Mittie, had died of typhoid fever eleven hours earlier at 3 a.m., in the same house. Distraught, Roosevelt left baby Alice in the care of his sister Bamie in New York City, retreating to the isolation of the rugged Dakotas to grieve. [4]

Diving headlong into the challenging lifestyle of the cowboy rancher, it was in North Dakota where Teddy Roosevelt not only found himself again, but also found healing and a new strength and purpose in life. He would later go on to say,

---

3 | Roosevelt wrote a short book entitled *The Strenuous Life*. I highly recommend it.
4 | He would return to reassume custody and parenting of his beloved Alice two years later.

"I have always said I would not have been President had it not been for my experience in North Dakota ... It was here that the romance of my life began."

Beyond Shallow Clichés

Ok, can I get on soapbox for just a second?

When it comes to the mysteries of how God works within the adversities of our lives, there are a couple of clichés that I just have to comment on. They are sayings that are well intended, and likely motivated by the Paul's words in Romans 8:28:

> *"And we know that in all things God works for the good of those who love him, who have been called according to his purpose."*

These are good words of encouragement written by Paul, especially when they are read and understood within their context. However, some unfortunate, homespun sayings have developed that, though well intended, do damage to the truth Paul is communicating.

Just silently nod your head "yes," if you have ever heard these:

> *"What doesn't kill you will make you stronger."*

> *and ...*

> *"God never gives you more than you can handle."*

Remember what I said about nodding your head if you have ever heard these? Now I want to you slap yourself if you have ever said these (just kidding – I think almost everyone has said some form of these at some point). Anyway ... moving on ...

The problem with clichés is that they generally only communicate a shallow form of the truth. The shallow encouragement offered by these two sayings can actually create great discouragement in people at deeper levels as they honestly wrestle with adversity.

Let me start with the first cliché ...

"What doesn't kill you will make you stronger."

Is this really, seriously true? No. It's not true in everyday life, and it isn't true biblically either. As one who has pastored people in one form or another the past 25 years, I can tell you without question that, for some people, the adversity they muddle through does NOT make them stronger. Often it shatters them. The state of one's faith and relationship with God can make all the difference in the recovery process. If the relationship is weak or non-existent with God to start, often the recovery never really happens or is anemic[5] at best. On the other hand, if the relationship is strong, recovery, and even strengthening is very possible.

A good example of this can be found in the life of C.S. Lewis. Lewis found love and companionship late in life – eventually marrying an American immigrant named Joy Davidman. Tragically, Joy was stricken with cancer soon after and, despite a brief remission, eventually succumbed to the horrible affliction. The death of his best friend pulled Lewis into a deep and dark period of grief. One of the ironic benefits of Lewis' grief was that during this period he kept a journal, which eventually was published as book entitled "A Grief Observed."[6]

The same man who earlier had once written, "Pain is God's megaphone to rouse a deaf world,"[7] now found himself in the throes of anguish. Lewis is breathtakingly honest as he pushes his way through the grief process. Looking to his creator, he questions, attacks and even mocks God with what many might find to be an almost blasphemous tone. Though he never questions the existence of God, he most certainly questions His goodness.

> *"Not that I am (I think) in much danger of ceasing to believe in God. The real danger is of coming to believe such dreadful things about Him. The conclusion I dread is not 'So there's no God after all,' but 'So this is what God's really like. Deceive yourself no longer."*

---

5 | I reserve the right to make a distinction here in the area of mental illness. One's ability to recover should never give people a license to judge – especially when mental illness is in play. Grace and prayerful intervention should fill the gap in such situations.
6 | Ironically he published the book under a pseudonym, N.W. Clerk, and was given many gift copies of it from people after Joy's death.
7 | From Lewis' book *The Problem of Pain.*

Pounding on his heavenly Father's chest until his energy is spent, Lewis finally begins to perceive shafts of light, among which are the realization that adversity such is this forces one into a more mature understanding and relationship with God.

> *"God has not been trying an experiment on my faith or love in order to find out their quality. He knew it already. It was I who didn't. In this trial He makes us occupy the dock, the witness box, and the bench all at once. He always knew that my temple was a house of cards. His only way of making me realize the fact was to knock it down."*

Biblically, we also see several examples of people who didn't emerge from adversity stronger.

- King Saul refuses to repent of his disobedience to the LORD, struggling with despair, and ultimately killing himself on the battle-field.

- Jonah wallows in anger and unforgiveness, despite the LORD's attempts to teach him mercy.

- Judas and Peter both betray Jesus. But unlike Peter, Judas yields to despair and kills himself before he can be offered the same forgiveness Peter later receives.

Adversity, in and of itself, does not necessarily make you stronger. However, adversity when submitted to the Lord, can make you stronger – a distinction Paul is careful to make in Romans 8, and a distinction we dare not leave aside.

And now for the second cliché ...

> *"God doesn't give you anything you can't handle."*

This is untrue for two really important reasons.

First, God DOES allow more than we can handle in order that we might learn humility. Seriously, if we could handle everything God gave us, then why would we need God? Our inability to handle everything reminds us that we need God, and that we shouldn't be so quick to judge others.

Years ago, before we even purchased our little ranch, Pam signed us up for horseback riding lessons. Pam is an Occupational Therapist by training, and she works with head injuries all the time. I think she was having some bad dreams about me flying of the rear end of a horse. Anyway …

After several weeks of training, one night, our teacher Marla decided to have us ride the horses bareback (no saddles). This would serve as a good test of our balance and budding skills, especially as we began to push the pace past a walk into a healthy trot. The horse I was riding was a wide, stout Morgan named HT (stands for High Tail). As we rode, I was actually doing pretty well – my balance was solid, and the faster trot was not presenting a problem. I was starting to feel like a Norwegian John Wayne.

Pam, and the other hand, was clearly struggling. I could see that her balance was shifting continuously, her seat (that equestrian language for "butt") never finding its home in the middle of her horse's back. Marla simultaneously offered encouragement to me, while vocalizing a steady stream of correction to Pam.

"This horseback riding thing isn't so hard …." I pridefully thought to myself. I even considered yelling some correction to Pam myself. But then I considered the health of our marriage, and thought the better of it. Still, I was definitely (if not quite literally) up on my high horse.

That's when God decided to remind me of a very important truth.

Just as I was considering what rodeo event HT and I were going to enter, Marla yelled out, "Ok … SWITCH HORSES!"

Without really thinking about it – I mounted Pam's horse Buck (thankfully his behavior was not indicative of his name). As I began riding Buck bareback I quickly came to the realization that he was a much different horse than HT. While HT was a wide Morgan, Buck was a skinny quarter horse. Riding HT bareback was like sitting in a Barcalounger (oh – there's that name again). Riding on Buck was like balancing your crotch on a seven-foot jackhammer and flipping the switch.[8]

---

8 | I seem to recall that Saul of Tarsus (Paul) had a similar experience of being knocked off his high horse in Acts 9.

It wasn't pretty. I managed to stay on but ... well, let's just say that having a third child probably wasn't going to be an option after that night. What was the lesson?

Never judge another person's ride
until you get on their horse.

Now ... the second reason God allows us experience more than we can handle? In a word: *community*.

Community is not merely a value God holds; community is at the very core of His identity.[9] God allows trials in our lives that exceed our ability to handle them so that we might learn to love and be loved.

It is not independence that characterizes the Kingdom of God, but interdependence.

We American's love going to the movies. We especially love the flawed and lonely hero, who saves the day while tragically spurning true love and relationship. It may come off as romantic on film, but it is a little like washing and waxing a Ferrari, but always refusing to actually drive it. The classic 70's band The Eagles wrote a song about such foolish figures entitled *Desperado*.

> *Desperado, why don't you come to your senses?*
> *You been out ridin' fences for so long now*
> *Oh you're a hard one*
> *I know that you got your reasons*
> *These things that are pleasin' you*
> *Can hurt you somehow*
>
> *Don't you draw the queen of diamonds boy*
> *She'll beat you if she's able*
> *You know the queen of hearts is always your best bet*
>
> *Now it seems to me some fine things*
> *Have been laid upon your table*
> *But you only want the ones that you can't get*

---

9 | When John says "God is love," he is not only saying God values love, he is revealing the mystery that community is at the very heart of the Trinity. (1 John 4:8).

Desperado, oh, you ain't gettin' no younger
Your pain and your hunger, they're drivin' you home
And freedom, oh freedom well, that's just some people talkin'
Your prison is walking through this world all alone

Don't your feet get cold in the winter time?
The sky won't snow and the sun won't shine

It's hard to tell the night time from the day
You're losin' all your highs and lows
Ain't it funny how the feeling goes away?

Desperado, why don't you come to your senses?
Come down from your fences, open the gate
It may be rainin', but there's a rainbow above you
You better let somebody love you, before it's too late[10]

Funny the places you find biblical truth. Though you will find, in some sense, heroes in the stories of scripture, what you won't find celebrated are isolated *desperados*.

- Abraham had Sarah
- Moses had Aaron
- David had Jonathon
- Esther had her uncle Mordecai
- Daniel had Shadrach, Meshach, and Abednego
- Elijah had Elisha
- Ruth had Naomi
- Ezra had Nehemia
- Mary had Joseph
- The other Mary had Martha
- Apollos had Priscilla and Aquilla
- Timothy had Paul

The pattern is not by accident. God gifts us with people to help us overcome adversity, and learn the highest values of His Kingdom even as he nurtures and refines our spiritual gifts.

---

10 | I would suggest you listen to the song on YouTube while you think on the lyrics.

Preparing for the Ultimate "Arrival"

Have you ever heard the phrase, "missing the forest for the trees"?

That's actually a pretty good cliché. The hidden gem of wisdom it teaches is that sometimes we miss the big picture because we are focusing on less important details. This is often true when it comes to the relationship between adversity and our pursuit of the spiritual gifts.

Many years ago, when my son Josh was a young lad, we signed him up for summer swimming lessons. The lessons were being held at the Elks Pool. Now, this pool was no modern water park. This pool was old-school. It had old-school diving boards, and a legitimate deep end (15 feet). It also had an old-school water slide – basically a knockoff of the classic playground version (old people: ever burn your butt on one of those?).

Josh took to the lessons pretty well – except for going down the slide. For some reason, he was just scared of it. The first couple of days, I didn't think much of it. But as the fear persisted, I determined that if I didn't find a way to help Josh overcome it, I would have my fatherhood card revoked.

If you have read my previous book, you know I am not averse to trying every tool in the parenting toolbox. In this case, I would resort to a good old-fashioned bribe. Josh's favorite restaurant in the whole wide world was a place called Space Aliens. He loved the food, but like any red-blooded American boy, he liked the game room even more.

On the final day of lessons, I promised him lunch at Space Aliens if he would go down the slide. He was one motivated kiddo.

As the end of the lesson came, the teacher herded the kids over toward the slide. Josh fell in line, awaiting his turn. I watched, a trickle of hope running through my heart. As he got to the base of the slide's ladder and squeezed his hands on the cold metal railing, Josh looked up as if to muster whatever amount of courage was hiding within his little frame.

Then he walked away.

Becoming quite animated, I hurried over to him, vocalizing intense bursts of encouragement to him through the chain-link fence. This scene repeated itself several times – right up to the final moment when this group's lessons needed to end in order to make room the next one.

"Josh!," I yelled, "You can do it. I know you can. Remember, if you do it we will go to Space Aliens!"

And then ... a miracle. Steeling himself one final time, Josh grabbed the ladder and made his way up to the top, perching his little butt on the peak of the slide.

"Go, go, go, go ....," yelled the other kids.

"Go, go, go, go ....," I echoed.

And then he did it. Eyes as wide as saucers, he launched himself down the half-pipe and splashed with abandon into the water. Bedlam ensued (at least that's how I remember it in my exaggerated Dad memory). I was so happy for him. To the casual bystander, it was just a boy going down the slide at the local pool. But to me, it was my son experiencing a life-changing moment of overcoming fear.

But that's not exactly how Josh saw it ...

As he burst forth from the deep, his arms held high in victory, I expected Josh to say something like, "I did it! I did it Dad! I'm not afraid anymore!"

But, I suppose that would be the Hollywood ending.

No ... Josh had something else on his mind. Rewind to reality.

Bursting forth from the deep, his arms held high in victory, Josh thundered with as much power as his little voice could carry, "I'm going to Space Aliens!" (OK – I admit, it did make me laugh).

As his dad, I was excited about the true reward of the moment – my son trusted me, and had overcome his fear. He had pushed through adversity. He was growing. He was tapping into his potential. He was discovering his strength. He was becoming a man.

Josh, on the other hand, was more focused on the smaller reward – an afternoon of pizza and games at his favorite eating establishment. Before him was a whole forest – but in his limited maturity he could only see the trees. Even now as I remember the moment with great sentimentality, I am reminded that we all often think gifts, goals and rewards are more important than the growth. But our heavenly father is ultimately much more pleased with the growth.

In Matthew 21, we find Jesus and disciples coming into Jerusalem to great fanfare. It is the week of Passover, and Jesus is being welcomed as a king. The disciples are excited – finally after seeing their master perform miracles of healing and casting out demons, he is accepting the worship and accolades they have been waiting upon. It is all very heady and exciting.

They think they have "arrived."

But their master knew better. He could see the forest, while they were distracted by the trees. He knew that their training was really just beginning, and on the verge of going to a whole new level. The disciples were focused on appropriating a temporary kingdom. Jesus was focused on training and shaping them to proclaim and inherit an eternal kingdom.

Resistance would come, and with it change. It would make them stronger. There would be no shortcuts.

And the world would never be the same.

Embrace with passion, faith and honesty whatever resistance your trainer brings your way. Remember, all other "arrivals" are just a grand rehearsal for the ultimate arrival.

Happy training.

Your Spiritual Gift is Not *Your* Spiritual Gift

"Do not be satisfied with God's calling or His gifts in your life. Be satisfied with Jesus Christ Himself."

Brother Yun, *The Heavenly Man: The Remarkable True Story of Chinese Christian Brother Yun*

You don't own your spiritual gift, God does.
He can give it – He can take it away.
Let's just get that straight before moving forward.

A Strange Life Lesson

Entering my 9th grade year at Simle Jr. High, something strange, unfamiliar, and totally unexpected happened; I became popular.

I had no idea how this happened. I definitely didn't see it coming. Maybe it had something to do with a growth spurt (I shot up 6 inches from 5'6 to 6'). Maybe it was that my basketball skills took a leap, and I was having the best year of my short career. Maybe it was because Ronald Reagan was elected president and the country was generally in a more optimistic mood. I don't know … but that's about how random it felt.

The moment when I realized something was up was in band one day. Our director, Mr. Anderson, would daily list the songs for practice on one of those black message boards with the press-on white letters. It was his custom to let some of the popular girls go into his office at the end of each class period and change the board for the next day and hang it up again. It had become a running joke that at least once every week, these girls would slip a message onto the board about the boys they thought were "hot." This had gone on for a couple of years, and it was always the same one or two boys who would be the object of their attention.

And then one day it happened. The girls went in the office … the board came back out and was hung up. I wasn't even paying attention. It took the simultaneous sound of laughter and a sharp elbow from my buddy Tracy to alert me to the seismic shift in reality ...

"RANDY UPGREN IS A HUNK!"

I couldn't believe my eyes. Was this real? When you have spent your whole life outside of such circles of popularity and attention what do you do with such a moment? All I could do was nervously laugh and hide my crimson face in my hands.

I mean just think about it ...

I had worked hard to become a good basketball player, and when it happened, I wasn't surprised, and I knew what to do with that gift.

I had worked hard to become a good trumpet player, and when it happened, I wasn't surprised, and I knew what to do with that gift.

I had worked hard to become a good student, and when the grades reflected that, I wasn't surprised, and I knew what to do with that gift.

But I didn't ask for popularity. Elevated status in the Jr. High universe was never something on my radar. Maybe it was a by-product of the other things – I didn't know. It was a complete surprise, and I had NO IDEA WHAT TO DO WITH THAT GIFT!

Did I parlay this new status into more exciting weekends with the "IN" crowd? No. Did I take advantage and start dating all the cheerleaders? No. (I liked girls but they scared the daylights out of me.)

Did I even attempt to use the position for good, like connecting this new circle of interested people with some of my other "average" friends? In other words, did I use it to build bridges between differing clicks of people? To my shame – No.

I just sat on this gift. I did nothing. Maybe I was scared the new group would discover I was really an imposter – that I wasn't as cool, or fun, or good looking as they thought.

Within six months I wasn't popular anymore. Without any fanfare I just sort of quietly drifted back to my original reality. To this day I have mixed feelings about the whole thing. But I also vowed to never let another opportunity like that, or of any sort, drift by without taking advantage in the right ways.

I think sometimes God gives us non-spiritual lessons in order to prepare us for more important spiritual opportunities later in life. I'll get to how that played out for me later in this book.

The Spiritual Gifts Are Dynamic, Not Static

Well known Christian leader and author Graham Cooke once said.

> "... we are learning to live in the paradox of God – to know that He is consistent, but He is also unpredictable. He is consistent in His nature – you always know where you are with God, but you seldom know what He is going to do next."[1]

I agree with this. We can find peace in the knowledge that God is rock-solid in his relational love for us. But a quick perusal through the Bible will quickly reveal that He is very unpredictable in his activity.

• In Abraham and Sarah, God chooses the poster children for the AARP to have a child and start a nation.

• In Gideon, God chooses a scared young man to win a great battle with only trumpets, torches and pots.

• A little shepherd boy named David takes down an undefeated giant with a sling shot.

• Rather than invade with power, God the creator enters into his creation quietly through a humble young virgin named Mary.

• God chooses the early churches' greatest enemy, a Pharisee named Saul of Tarsus, to become its greatest evangelist.

---

1 | From a sermon entitled "The Nature of God."

This is just a small sampling of the many examples of God's unpredictable movements. God's priority always lies in whatever activity it takes to bring about his Kingdom. This activity often surprises our human expectations or assumptions. This is why, although it is good to seek and exercise our spiritual gifting, it is also paramount that we always hold onto these gifts lightly.

In any given moment, God's work may require of you the highest degree of your spiritual gifting, or, a humble season of quiet waiting and inactivity.

It is not about our gifting, but about God's plan.

Now having said that, this doesn't mean that God's management of our spiritual gifting is random. Several helpful principles can be discerned from the pages of scripture.

Principles Regarding God's Provision of Gifts

1. God bestows His Holy Spirit, and the gifts that come with Him, as we move obediently in faith

Too often, we want to experience our spiritual giftedness exactly backwards from the way God wants. We want God to provide, and then we will obey. God wants us to obey, trusting that He will provide. A couple of great biblical examples of this can be found in Exodus 14 and Joshua 3. Both stories have to do with the people of Israel crossing over water (The Red Sea and the Jordan River).

In Exodus 14, the Hebrews were trapped and in panic mode, fearing they were about to die at the hands of Pharaoh. Moses comforts them:

"Moses answered the people, "Do not be afraid. Stand firm and you will see the deliverance the Lord will bring you today. The Egyptians you see today you will never see again. The Lord will fight for you; you need only to be still."

Then the Lord said to Moses, **"Why are you crying out to me?** Tell the Israelites to move on. Raise your staff and stretch out your hand over the sea to divide the water so that the Israelites can go through the sea on dry ground."

In Joshua 3, the great multitude of Israel needed to cross the Jordan River, which at the time was at flood stage. Rather than part the river before moving, God orders a strangely familiar edict:

"Tell the priests who carry the Ark of the Covenant: 'When you reach the edge of the Jordan's waters, go and stand in the river.' ... Now the Jordan is at flood stage all during harvest. Yet as soon as the priests who carried the ark reached the Jordan and their feet touched the water's edge, the water from upstream stopped flowing."

Notice the pattern. God desires his people to trust him and walk in obedience even before he provides and moves on their behalf.

This is also the principle behind the financial obedience of tithing. We give back to God ten percent of our resources out of obedience, acknowledging that He is the source of our well-being, and will continue to be faithful in provision. I believe this is also why we saw Jesus respond so warmly to the Centurian's request to heal his servant. Though hated by the Jews as a Roman occupier, this soldier demonstrated the kind of proactive faith God delights in.[2]

2. God provides gifting according to circumstances

The power of God is especially moved when people seek to respond to need, regardless of whether they feel gifted. The Spirit of God can move even more freely and explosively through the heart of a person whose agenda is in perfect alignment with God's. Charles Hadden Spurgeon put it beautifully:

"Man is a fallen star till he is right with heaven: he is out of order with himself and all around him till he occupies his true place in relation to God. When he serves God, he has reached that point where he doth serve himself best, and enjoys himself

2 | Matthew 8:5-13

most. It is man's honour, it is man's joy, it is man's heaven, to live unto God."[3]

Probably the most dramatic example of this is found when Jesus sends out the 72 disciples to share the Gospel. Ordered to take nothing of provision with them, the men return dumbfounded by how God provided not only for their needs, but also empowered them with the gifts of preaching, teaching, exorcism and healing.

> *"The seventy-two returned with joy and said, "Lord, even the demons submit to us in your name."[4]*

An interesting example of this occurred at my church on an Easter morning many years ago. I had just finished my seminary degree and been ordained as a pastor. This increased the number of pastors at our church at that time to three. An abundance of clergy! However, on that day, what we did not have was an abundance of nursery workers. Actually we didn't have any. And so me and the other associate pastor (Scott Bauman) spent the morning rocking babies, adjusting burp rags, changing diapers, and wiping off spit up from our suits. Nursery wasn't our training – or even our calling – but it was the need that day, and we were available. I don't know if we received any specific spiritual gift that morning – but I do believe that because we chose to humble ourselves, God responded by strengthening the gift of leadership in us as a team.

3. God grows gifting in those who use it

This comes right out of the parable of the Talents taught by Jesus in Matthew 25:

> *"Now after a long time the master of those servants came and settled accounts with them. And he who had received the five talents came forward, bringing five talents more, saying, 'Master, you delivered to me five talents; here I have made five talents more.' His master said to him, 'Well done, good and faithful servant. **You have been faithful over a little; I will set you over much.** Enter into the joy of your master.' And he also who had the two talents came forward, saying, 'Master, you delivered to me two talents; here I have made two talents*

---

3 | From his essay *Humility and How to Get It*
4 | Luke 10:1-24

more.' His master said to him, **'Well done, good and faithful servant. You have been faithful over a little; I will set you over much.** Enter into the joy of your master.'"

St. Peter might be the most compelling example of how such gifting grows in its power over time through use. The same disciple that denied Jesus, would eventually lead the church (along with Paul) to the very temple steps of Caesar himself. Emperor Nero personally ordered the execution of Peter; a crucifixion which Peter request be performed upside down in reverence to his master. The church Father Tertullian attests to this:

> *"How fortunate is this Church for which the Apostles have poured out their whole teaching with their blood, where Peter has emulated the Passion of the Lord ..."[5]*

Principles Regarding God's Re-Direction of Gifts

This principle is fairly straightforward. Sometimes God intervenes in the life of someone in order to reorient and spiritually animate their natural gifts and passions toward his Kingdom.

The most striking and obvious biblical example of this is the Apostle Paul. If ever anyone ever underwent a paradigm shift it was Paul. Formerly known as Saul of Tarsus, Paul's religious qualifications were beyond question.

> *"... circumcised on the eighth day, of the people of Israel, of the tribe of Benjamin, a Hebrew of Hebrews; in regard to the law, a Pharisee; as for zeal, persecuting the church; as for righteousness based on the law, faultless. I am a Jew, born in Tarsus of Cilicia, but brought up in this city. I studied under Gamaliel and was thoroughly trained in the law of our ancestors. I was just as zealous for God as any of you are today."[6]*

There was just one problem: he hated Jesus and the early church and was fighting against the God he thought he was serving.

> *"As he neared Damascus on his journey, suddenly a light from*

5 | *De Prascriptione 36*
6 | Acts 22:2-3

heaven flashed around him. He fell to the ground and heard a voice say to him, "Saul, Saul, why do you persecute me?"

"Who are you, Lord?" Saul asked.

"I am Jesus, whom you are persecuting," he replied.

"Now get up and go into the city, and you will be told what you must do."[7]

Paul would undergo one of the greatest turnarounds in history. It wasn't so much that he needed a complete memory wipe of all he learned and knew, but more that he needed to see everything he learned and knew through new eyes (in his case quite literally). Once he understood that the God of Moses had come in the flesh as Jesus to make sacrifice for salvation, Paul became unstoppable.

His natural gifts became animated by the Holy Spirit, and the man who once swore to destroy the followers of Jesus would himself become the greatest preacher of all time.

> **"But whatever were gains to me I now consider loss for the sake of Christ.** *What is more, I consider everything a loss because of the surpassing worth of knowing Christ Jesus my Lord ..."[8]*

Principles Regarding God Withholding Spiritual Gifts

I realize this is not the most comfortable of principles to discuss. But it is real. Remember the gifts of the Spirit are not innately ours. They are God's to give or withhold as He sees fit. We are reminded that the concept stands solidly in Jesus' parable of the Talents in Matthew 25. The last time we looked at that story it was to observe how the master multiplied the talents of those who used them. This time we see the opposite principle at work in the final servant:

"Then the man who had received one bag of gold came.

7 | Acts 9:3-9
8 | Philippians 3:7-9

'Master,' he said, 'I knew that you are a hard man, harvesting where you have not sown and gathering where you have not scattered seed. So I was afraid and went out and hid your gold in the ground. See, here is what belongs to you.'

"His master replied, 'You wicked, lazy servant! So you knew that I harvest where I have not sown and gather where I have not scattered seed? Well then, you should have put my money on deposit with the bankers, so that when I returned I would have received it back with interest.'

"'So take the bag of gold from him and give it to the one who has ten bags. For whoever has will be given more, and they will have an abundance. **Whoever does not have, even what they have will be taken from them."**

Three different reasons for the withholding of God's presence and/or gifts seem to be present in scripture. In this story the first among our three reasons is the lesson: disobedience to the command of the master.

One doesn't have to go far in the Bible to find three dramatic examples of this: Samson, King Saul, and King Solomon. All three were anointed with the Spirit and gifted to lead, and all three squandered this gift in different ways.

Samson was a consecrated Nazirite. His strength lay in the seven uncut braids of his hair. His strength was renown and, called as a judge to protect Israel from the hate Philistines, Samson became a marked man. His appetites for female companionship lay the groundwork for the loss of his gift. After falling is love with a woman named Delilah, Samson eventually spills the beans on the secret of his strength. The conniving Delilah springs a trap, and Samson discovers the hard way, that it is possible to lose the gifting and presence of the LORD.

"He awoke from his sleep and thought, "I'll go out as before and shake myself free." **But he did not know that the Lord had left him.**

"Then the Philistines seized him, gouged out his eyes and took him down to Gaza. Binding him with bronze shackles, they set him to grinding grain in the prison."

King Saul begins to compromise on the commands of the LORD; he fudges on the spoils of battle, he fails to wait on the prophet Samuel before an important battle, and worst of all, he employs a medium to bring Samuel back from the dead to advise him. No wonder God ordered the anointing of David king before Saul was even dead! Ultimately the LORD is displeased and withdraws his presence from him.

> **"Now the Spirit of the LORD had departed from Saul,** and an evil spirit from the LORD tormented him."[9]

King Solomon benefited from the reign, repentance, and faithful heart of his father David. Solomon inherited the united kingdom of Israel and was blessed directly by the LORD with the gift of wisdom. However, sometimes success is the worst thing for a person, and Solomon became complacent in his relationship with the LORD, ultimately disobeying the command not to intermarry with foreign women and thus stray and worship their gods.

> "The Lord became angry with Solomon because his heart had turned away from the Lord, the God of Israel, who had appeared to him twice. Although he had forbidden Solomon to follow other gods, Solomon did not keep the Lord's command. So the Lord said to Solomon, 'Since this is your attitude and you have not kept my covenant and my decrees, which I commanded you, I will most certainly tear the kingdom away from you and give it to one of your subordinates.'"[10]

The wisdom that once made Solomon famous the world over, now haunted him. The book of Ecclesiastes records Solomon's tortured questions as his wisdom, absent from the Spirit of the LORD, forces him to question the meaning of everything. Ultimately a ray of hope shines through when at the conclusion of the book, Solomon acknowledges that meaning is only found in serving God.

> "Now all has been heard;
> here is the conclusion of the matter:
> Fear God and keep his commandments,
> for this is the duty of all mankind.

---

9 | I Samuel 16:14
10 | 1 Kings 11

For God will bring every deed into judgment,
including every hidden thing,
whether it is good or evil."

A second reason God may withhold his gifting or presence has to do with faith building. There are times that, in order to strengthen our faith and priorities, God may withhold what seems to be good so that we don't begin to confuse the gifts with the giver himself.

God wants us to love Him and use his gifts, not love his gifts and use Him.

This is a very difficult lesson, and many people automatically assume when they find themselves in this "wilderness" (Yes, Jesus knows this place too), it is because they have done something wrong before the Lord. But this is not always the case.

The Lord withheld from the Apostle Paul relief from an affliction he called "a thorn in the flesh."[11] We aren't sure what this was – maybe a moral struggle, perhaps continued issues with his eyesight – we don't know for sure. What we do know is that Paul repeatedly asked the Lord for help.

The Lord said, "No."

How easy would it have been for Paul to throw a tantrum, whining to God about how faithfully he had served Him, or how much he had sacrificed. I personally probably would've just jumped to the bargaining stage, offering to give up Twinkies in exchange. Twinkies – yes. A White Chocolate Mocha Latte – no. Anyway ...

In response to this rejection, Paul writes some of the most profound words of all of literature. Instead of healing, the Lord offers wisdom – a wisdom we would all do well to cling to:

> *"Therefore, in order to keep me from becoming conceited, I was given a thorn in my flesh, a messenger of Satan, to torment me. Three times I pleaded with the Lord to take it away from me.*
>
> *"But he said to me, 'My grace is sufficient for you, for my power is made perfect in weakness.' Therefore I will boast*

---

11 | 2 Corinthians 12

all the more gladly about my weaknesses, so that Christ's power may rest on me. That is why, for Christ's sake, I delight in weaknesses, in insults, in hardships, in persecutions, in difficulties. For when I am weak, then I am strong."

Finally, the third reason God may withhold his presence or gifting is so that you will embrace the reality that it may be time to make room for a new leader. For an immature person, this process can get really ugly. But for the mature person, this process can be a gentle and nuanced way to make room for the next person God wants to use, and even move you to your own next stage of giftedness.

Elijah mentored and moved over for Elisha. The Spirit now needed to work in new ways among the people. Both came battling idolatry and calling the people back to the LORD. However, just as Elijah did so with fire and miracles of judgment, so his successor Elisha did so with mercy. The two of them served as a tandem of Law and Gospel. Scholar HJ Howat writes,

> "The miracles wrought by the two prophets form another interesting point of contrast between Elijah and Elisha. It is noticeable that Elisha wrought twice as many miracles as Elijah did, suggesting the inference that the parting request had been complied with to the letter: 'And Elisha said, I pray thee let a double portion of thy spirit be upon me.'

> "On his introduction to work, Elijah begins with a miracle – the emblem of so much of his future career – a miracle of judgment: 'There shall not be dew nor rain these years,' referring to the drought, 'but according to My word.' Elisha begins with a miracle – the emblem also of so much of his future career – but it is a miracle of mercy: 'There shall not be from thence,' speaking of the bitter waters of Jericho sweetened, 'any more death or barren land.'

> "The miracles of Elisha, in fact, remind us very much of the miracles of Christ – miracles of beneficence. The very grave of Elisha wrought a miracle that reads very like a miracle of Christ, for 'when the man was let down and touched the bones of Elisha, he revived and stood up on his feet.'"[12]

---

12 | Article from Biblehub.com

A Founding Father Submits
to His Divine Father

This summer of 2015, I had the privilege to take my family to Washington, DC, to learn more about the Christian heritage of the great American experiment. It was absolutely amazing.

While there, our family had the pleasure of visiting Mount Vernon, the home of George Washington. I don't know anyone who would dispute that George Washington was amazingly gifted for leadership. Many may not think that gifting had anything to do with God, but I can assure you, Washington himself absolutely believed the Almighty was the sole provider of his wisdom and protector of the young nation.

> *"I am sure there never was a people, who had more reason to acknowledge a divine interposition in their affairs, than those of the United States; and I should be pained to believe, that they have forgotten that agency, which was so often manifested during our revolution, or that they failed to consider the omnipotence of that God, who is alone able to protect them."*
> **Letter to John Armstrong, 11 March 1782**

Many great achievements pepper our first president's career. However, it was what he didn't do that marked him as perhaps one of the greatest leaders of recorded history. Despite some efforts to make him emperor, George Washington became the first man in history to willingly step down from significant power, not once, but twice. Washington's great adversary, King George III, asked his American painter, Benjamin West, what Washington would do after winning independence. West replied, "They say he will return to his farm."

"If he does that," the incredulous monarch said, "he will be the greatest man in the world."[13]

George Washington understood from the beginning that all things rested on the goodness and mercy of God himself. This included Washington's precious gifts of wisdom and leadership from which

---

13 | David Boaz, *The Man Who Would Not Be King*, Cato Institute, 2006

we all still benefit today. When the moment arrived he knew what to do with the gifts and opportunities thrust upon him – but he also knew to hold them lightly – and when the time came, to let them go.

Love God and use his gifts.

Let service and need shape your actions, not your ego.

Let's see ... what did Jesus say again? Oh, yea ...

> "Seek first the Kingdom of God, and all these things will be added unto you."

This is especially true of the spiritual gifts.

Remember, they are not yours.

But what an amazing privilege to use them as God sees fit.

When To Push Forward In Faith

It is not the critic who counts; not the man who points out how the strong man stumbles, or where the doer of deeds could have done them better. The credit belongs to the man who is actually in the arena, whose face is marred by dust and sweat and blood; who strives valiantly; who errs, who comes short again and again, because there is no effort without error and shortcoming; but who does actually strive to do the deeds; who knows great enthusiasms, the great devotions; who spends himself in a worthy cause; who at the best knows in the end the triumph of high achievement, and who at the worst, if he fails, at least fails while daring greatly, so that his place shall never be with those cold and timid souls who neither know victory nor defeat.

President Theodore Roosevelt

Do you remember when you learned to ride a bicycle?

If your experience was anything like mine, it probably involved a lot of excitement, nervousness, wobbling, yelling, falling, and skinned knees or elbows. I remember I learned on a stretch of sidewalk that had a large rock retaining wall on one side. This was probably not the most brilliant strategic decision my dad made in the whole endeavor ...

However, no matter where you learned, what kind of bike you used, or who helped you, there was one element of the learning process that was universally true for ALL of us ...

Forward movement.

You can't ride a bike unless you are moving forward. For that matter, you can't steer a bike if you are not moving forward.

Without forward motion you cannot learn.
Without forward motion you cannot go anywhere.

There are too many people in God's church seeking His will, but refusing to move forward. It is as if they are working really hard to just balance on a motionless bicycle, crying out to God to steer them in the right direction, and then getting frustrated with this same God when nothing happens.

This understanding of calling and giftedness is actually a form of idolatry. It is a form of discipleship without actual faith. We turn a deaf ear toward God's call, defaulting toward our comfort zone, and then wonder why our spiritual lives seem hollow and unfulfilling. It is as if we are spending the day at an amazing amusement park surrounded by exciting roller coasters, but all we do is walk around and eat cheese curds.

Meet RJ.

I have known him pretty much his whole life. He is one of my oldest son's best friends. RJ is an amazing young man, but has not generally had his dad in his life to guide him in some of the more masculine arts. His mom is amazing, a true example of the heroic single parent. In many ways I have had the honor of being a surrogate dad to RJ.[1] This aspect of our relationship played itself out in a humorous way one year.

Valley Fair in Shakopee, Minnesota, is a classic American amusement park. Among all of the attractions are some of this country's most intense roller coasters. Several years ago, I was helping to lead a middle school church mission trip to the area. After a hard week of work, Valley Fair was our play day. I spent the morning with a group of guys, including my own two boys, exploring the park – including sampling these metal monsters of the midway. By 11:30 a.m., we took a break for lunch.

That's when I saw him.

It was RJ, apparently having spent the entire morning with a group of girls. All of them were wearing these goofy hats. Now, I mean no offense to my female readers when I say this ... but the whole scene just looked so ... feminine.

My oldest son Josh, looking at the picture, uttered ... "What the ....?"

---

1 | RJ would himself tell you this – I am not being presumptive.

My youngest son Jordan elbowed me, "Dad we gotta grab him…"
A rescue operation ensued.[2]

Shoving a ham sandwich into his hands, we quietly but forcefully swooped in on the group and kidnapped RJ from the estrogen-laden flock.

"Come on RJ … we're going on the coasters!" I said, leaving no negotiation as to our agenda.

"What? …Really? …uh .. I don't know … never been on those … not sure if I'm comfortable with that ….," RJ stuttered in nervous response.[2]

"No … you're going. Your time has come buddy. Your brothers are here with you. You will be fine … actually you will be more than fine," I insisted.

Now … I know what some of you are thinking. "How dare you bully this kid into doing something he doesn't want to do?" I understand. But I need you to understand that in some sense the masculine identity of this young man was at stake. Sometimes we need a trusted mentor to push us past our fears and discover new aspects of our character and strength. Some of you might be thinking of this as just a roller coaster ride, but I was thinking about a young man who needed, as Roosevelt put it, to quit being a spectator and start being a participant.

> " … who at the best knows in the end the triumph of high achievement, and who at the worst, if he fails, at least fails while daring greatly, so that his place shall never be with those cold and timid souls who neither know victory nor defeat."

Learning to dare greatly in the little things prepares us to dare greatly in the big things.

We started with the most mellow coaster. It was called the Corkscrew. It was moderately fast, but it also took the rider on a series of corkscrew maneuvers and upside down flips. I had RJ sit next to me and coached him through what to expect as the

---

2 | I have no problem with guys hanging out with girls. But there are just some times when guys need to be around other guys. Especially in cases where guys are in need of male companionship and mentoring.

cars clinked heavily and started moving. RJ was pretty much just holding his breath ... until we hit Mach 1.

The one-minute ride was a blur – a visual and auditory watercolor of screams and laughter. At the close of the ride, RJ didn't just get out of the coaster car – he exploded out of it – years of pent up testosterone viscerally rupturing out of his body in a volcanic celebration of victory. It was as if he was a human soda pop bottle that had been shaken over and over again, and now finally opened. I have never seen someone so happily hyped following a coaster experience. He didn't just enjoy the ride – he needed the ride.

The truth is we all need the ride. We were made for it.

A Divine Collision of Meaning

You were made for more than just the treadmill of survival. You were made for more than just the shallow circle of entertaining yourself.

Frederich Buechner said, "Calling is the place where your deep gladness meets the world's deep need."

Let that sink in for a moment. Do you know that place? Have you visited it? Have you dreamed of such a place? Do you feel your heart drawn to it?

This is more than mere self-fulfillment. This is a call to greatness within the scope of God's vision – because there are places of need in this world that can benefit from what you are passionate about.

The key word is "need." God has shaped us and called us to meet needs in order that Jesus' prayer might come true ... "Thy Kingdom come, thy will be done, on earth as it is in heaven."

This is the believer's destiny. That's not just me blowing smoke. It's woven into the precious vision of God.

"For we are God's handiwork, created in Christ Jesus to do good works, which God prepared in advance for us to do."[3]

The world needed light from the darkness of idolatry, so God called Abraham.

The people of Egypt and the family of Jacob needed refuge from famine, so God called Joseph.

The Hebrews needed freedom from Pharoah's hand, so God called Moses.

The Jews needed salvation from the genocidal plot of Haman, so God called Esther.

The Israelites needed relief from the oppression of the Midianites, so God called Gideon.

The people of Israel needed to be called back into covenant with God again, so God called Amos.

The people needed salvation from sin, so God called Mary.

The world needed the freedom of the Gospel, so God called Paul.

There is a kind of forward motion to the calling of God. The calling is a work of grace in at least two aspects. One aspect is that to answer the call and start moving is already a defined victory. It is not ultimately achievement or speed that God is most pleased with – it is movement – those first steps of walking in trust with him. This is the vertical blessing – our relationship with God deepens and becomes more tangible.

The other aspect of grace is that as you allow God to work you and shape you, He will begin to draw others to Himself through you. This is the horizontal blessing. It is important not to try to analyze this part of the blessing too much. It works at levels that

---

3 | Ephesians 2:10

we are often unable to see or understand. We must rest in the simple obedience of trusting our master, celebrating the small victories gratefully as He chooses to reveal them to us.[4]

The only failure occurs when, after sensing a calling, we turn the other way. Author and business consultant Arthur Miller rebukes this response quite strongly,

> "It is wrong, it is sin, to accept or remain in a position that you know is a mismatch for you. Perhaps that's a form of sin you've never even considered – the sin of staying in the wrong job. But God did not place you on this earth to waste away your years in labor that does not employ his design or purpose for your life, no matter how much you may be getting paid for it."[5]

Discerning the Call of God: Restlessness, Need, Opportunity & Fit, Risk

Discerning whether God might be calling you into this new reality of forward motion can be a little intimidating. Part of the reason why so many don't respond to their calling is that they are afraid of making a wrong move and ending up on the wrong path. We will address that in a later chapter.

I have found that the act of listening is extremely important in the discernment process (which, by the way, doesn't come naturally to loud-mouthed preachers). The best way to do this is to process some basic questions prayerfully and in the guidance of those you trust.

Question #1:
Do you sense a persistent restlessness in your life right now?

This restlessness could be rooted in a couple of different places.

One would be that you just feel like your life doesn't fit, like a shoe that's one size too small. Perhaps you are not passionate about the focus of your work or vocation? Perhaps you feel like you are capable of contributing more than you are allowed?

---

4 | A great read on this concept is *A Long Slow Obedience in the Same Direction* by Eugene Peterson.
5 | *The Power of Uniqueness.*

Perhaps you find yourself day-dreaming about other possibilities on an annoyingly consistent basis?

Another root cause could exist at a much deeper level. Are you actually quite good at your vocation, finding that it fits your skills and education, but still find that it leaves you feeling empty? In other words, its not so much about "fit" as it is about meaning. Are you haunted by the knowledge that your impact and sense of calling might be realized more fully in a place that requires you to take a pay cut – to make a sacrifice of your comfort zone?

In my previous book, "The End is The Beginning," I elaborated about how sometimes the process of recognizing and responding to calling is not some pure "Hallelujah" moment of euphoria, but rather an agonizing wrestling with God. I shared the story of Richard Stearns, and how his calling extricated him from the comfortable life of a China executive to CEO of World Vision. Richard describes the moment God came a calling:

> "Several months after becoming a Christian, I was newly engaged to Reneé. As we were planning our wedding and our life together, she suggested that we go to a department store to register for our china, crystal, and silver. My self-righteous response was an indication of just how my newfound faith was integrating into my life: 'As long as there are children starving in the world, we're not going to own fine china, crystal, and silver.'

> "Perhaps you can see God's sense of irony in my becoming president of America's premier fine tableware company a couple of decades later. So when I answered that phone call from World Vision in January 1998, I knew that God was on the other end of the line. It was his voice I heard, not the recruiter's: **Rich, do you remember that idealistic young man in 1974 who was so passionate about starving children that he would not even fill out a wedding registry? Take a good look at yourself now. Do you see what you've become? But, Rich, if you still care about those children, I have a job I want you to do."**

Question #2:
Is there a need in the world that persistently haunts you?
Mother Theresa could not ignore the unjust caste system of India.

Charles Colson could not leave his fellow prisoners behind without sharing the Gospel. Kim and Troy Meeder couldn't ignore broken horses, and then noticed how these broken horses could help mend broken kids.

Nehemiah couldn't ignore Jerusalem's need for walls to keep her safe while she reestablished herself as a nation. The midwives couldn't ignore their calling to save the male Hebrew babies – even in defiance of Pharaoh's orders.

The list goes on and on ... the world says to ignore your pain, and the pain in the world. But God will move you to consider that this just might be the starting point of your calling and gifting. We will also talk about the role of pain in a later chapter.

Question #3:
Has your soul been awakened by an opportunity that fits you?

These opportunities just may be God giving you the opportunity to fulfill your destiny. Be careful though – not every opportunity is a calling from God! Filter every opportunity through the grid of the following questions:

- What do I enjoy doing for its own sake?
- What do I avoid doing? Why?
- For what do I wish to be remembered?
- How might the offer of money or promotion sidetrack me from my true calling?
- What would my life look like if it turned out well?[6]
- Does this work meet a significant need in the world?
- Is this work in alignment with the values and principles of Jesus?

Do the answers to these questions seem to harmonize with each other, even if it might mean a loss of income, status, or comfort?

In particular, pay attention to the first two questions as they can bring significant light to our motives. I recently was strongly

---

6 | Taken in part from John Ortberg's book *If You Want To Walk on Water You Have to Get Out of the Boat.* P. 68.

encouraged to apply for a position that on the surface seemed like the classic "upward mobility" opportunity. However, after sifting through the above questions with trusted people in my life, I realized I would have been taking the position for the wrong reasons, largely doing work I didn't enjoy, and entering into an unhealthy situation. Despite a substantial increase in income and status, I decided to not apply for the position.

Fit and motive count for almost everything. Researcher Mihaly Csikszentmihalyi (good luck pronouncing that), did a study involving two hundred artists nearly two decades after they left art school. He found that it was those students who enjoyed painting for its own sake that were overwhelmingly likely to become the most successful painters. Those drawn to art school in hopes of wealth or fame drifted away to other professions. Said Csikszentmihalyi, "Painters must want to paint above all else. If the artist in front of the canvas begins to wonder how much he will sell it for, or what the critics will think of it, he won't be able to pursue original avenues. Creative achievements depend on single-minded immersion."

Question #4:
Is the price of inaction acceptable to you at this stage of your life?

This is an assessment of risk vs. regret. – What are the risks involved with moving forward (considerable as they might be), when compared with the potential regrets involved with not moving forward

The classic Rocking Chair test can be helpful in answering this question. When you are very old and sitting on your rocking chair, might you regret not pursuing this path? This isn't a set-up. The season of life you are in might play a big role in your answer – and remember the answers are not limited to "yes" and "no." "Wait" is another possibility. So is "Part time," or "As a side pursuit." For people who are in the child-rearing years, some of these other options might be helpful possibilities. Moving forward might not take the form of an already-existing new job, but rather a new start-up such as starting a small non-profit.

I will never forget New Years Eve, 2011. We were having dinner at my in-laws and enjoying some fairly casual conversation. Someone brought the idea of making New Year's resolutions, but I dismissed it because, in general, we were not in the habit of proclaiming promises we were not likely to keep.

But then my wife, Pam, spoke up. "I'm making a resolution. This year Providence Ranch Ministries is going to become an official non-profit organization." Up until that point, Pam and I were doing an annual horse camp for the kids in our church – but after a couple of years it was clear the demand was much bigger than that – especially among families who had special needs kids.

Even though the idea of running her own non-profit organization scared her half to death, Pam shared that she felt that it was time to give the little ministry we had started a chance to grow and more significantly be a blessing to families. This was a big deal. You see, Pam would be the first to admit that she tends to be pretty risk averse – and here she was, putting it on the line, announcing it to the whole family.

I couldn't have been more proud of her. Six seasons later, though we are still rather small – we are reaching 50-60 kids and their families per season. Providence Ranch Ministries currently works in partnership with several other organizations in the Bismarck area, and offers all of its programs free of charge. Though Pam would never say this ... it is true – she has become dangerous in all the right ways, and I'm proud to serve alongside her.[7]

Moving Within God's Call:
No Stones Unturned

When moving forward within the flow of God's call, it is extremely important to eliminate all assumptions about how God may, or may not work. If there is one thing I have learned in twenty-five years of ministry, it's that you never know from what direction help, support, opportunity, or financial resourcing may come from. In light of this I cannot emphasize enough the idea of leaving no stones unturned. Movement doesn't stop until this has happened.

This doesn't mean you aren't depending upon God – quite the opposite. What it means is that you refuse to limit the way God might work by your own human boundaries. As you walk with God

---

7 | If you would like to know more about Providence Ranch Ministries or donate to our ministries go to providenceranchnd.com.

in calling you must get comfortable with the idea that you don't know what you don't know! In light of this I recommend you keep front and center the following principles:

- People are your greatest resource. People want to be involved in things that God is doing. Don't place limitations on how people can help you move forward in your pursuit of your calling.

- Get over your shyness about asking for help. People who have resources are looking for worthy causes to support.

- When seeking resources, never assume someone will say "No." Broaden your search to include every possibility. It's OK for people to say "no," and for you to hear it – but press on trusting that somewhere in the mix is a "yes."

- As much as possible, create win-win relationships with people and/or organizations that support you. You are not called to be a parasite. Look for ways to bless and serve those who support you.

- Never lose sight of your ethics. Never compromise your soul for support.

- Be patient. Slow progress is often better than fast progress. Remember what we learned in previous chapters – God wants to grow your character in order to maximize the potential of your gifting. Understand that failure is part of the process, and embrace the role it plays in your maturity.

- Be flexible. The path will likely NOT be exactly as you expect. As you move forward you will have discoveries about yourself and the process that surprise you. You may not end up where you expect – but you will end up where God wants you.

In his delightful book on calling and gifting, *The Dream Giver*, Bruce Wilkenson shares a story about an encounter he and his wife had with a waitress named Sonja that illustrates what I've been describing.

" 'Are you doing what you've always wished you could be doing?'

"(Sonja) looked at me questioningly. 'What do you mean?' she asked.

"I said, "Well, maybe you are doing your dream, and that would be terrific. But I wonder, do you have a Big Dream inside your heart that hasn't come true yet?"

"Sonja thought for a moment. Then she said, 'My mother is a nurse. My sister is a nurse. And I always dreamed of becoming a nurse.'

"'Would you have been a good nurse?' I asked.

"Sonja became emotional. 'I would have been a really good nurse,' she said softly.

"'Would you like to be a nurse at this very moment?' I asked.

"'Yes,' she said.

"So I took another risk. 'Do you happen to believe that God wants you to be a nurse?' I asked.

"She looked away for a minute, then said, 'I think so.'

"'If God wants you to be a nurse, then there must be a way for you to be one,' I said. 'What has stopped you?'

"Sonja listed the reasons: an education cut short by marriage, then two children, then the demands of raising a family. 'Now it's impossible,' she said. 'It's too late.' I heard the sadness in her voice.

"'What would have to happen for you to become a nurse?" 'I asked.

"'We don't have enough money,' she said. 'I can't afford a babysitter, so I can't go to school.'

"'So if you had a babysitter, you would go to school?' I asked.

"'Yes,' she said, without hesitation.

"... Then I took a risk. 'Sonja, I believe there's somebody in your life who cares about you and would babysit your children for free. Who is that person?'

"Sonja thought for a moment, then her face lit up. 'It's my mother!" she exclaimed. 'She just retired two months ago! She loves her grandchildren. And she's always wanted me to have my dream. She'd babysit my kids for free if I just asked her!'

"While she spoke, her eyes brimmed with tears. Mine did, too. Anytime I see someone else's dream surfacing, I'm deeply touched, because I know how sad it is not to be able to live your dream.

"Without even taking our order, Sonja slid in next to a friend at another table to announce that she was going back to school. 'I'm going to be a nurse!' she said with tears of joy."

Scenarios like this play out everyday in the world.

Why not you?

Has God been calling you?

Are you feeling restless, hollow, underutilized and haunted?

It may be time for you to move. It may not be.

But why not at least vet out the question?

Get on the bike. Start moving.

After-all ...God make you for the ride.

When To Wait On God

*Timing is so important! If you are going to be
successful in dance, you must be able to
respond to rhythm and timing. It's the same
in the Spirit. People who don't understand
God's timing can become spiritually spastic,
trying to make the right things happen at
the wrong time. They don't get His rhythm
– and everyone can tell they are out of step. They birth things
prematurely, threatening the very lives of their God-given
dreams.*

T.D. Jakes, *What Christians Want to Know*

In Mexico, they call it Montezuma's revenge; intense nausea, vomiting, and diarrhea brought on by bacterial contamination. Thankfully, I have never experienced this firsthand.

However, I have seen this firsthand.

The summer of 1994 I was leading a dozen Sr. High youth on a mission trip to Matamoros, Mexico. After managing the insanity of crossing the border, our group joined five other groups from across the United States for a memorable week of service and making new friends. However, the service and new friendships weren't the only things that were memorable.

One of the most strongly emphasized instructions our hosts gave us was not to drink the water. I know … I know … you are thinking, "Well, of course, any idiot who goes to Mexico knows that". Remember we are talking about teenagers … and some adults …. Anyway….

Not only were we to not drink the water, we were to not even brush our teeth with it. In light of this, our hosts brought in bottled water for these purposes on a daily basis. However, one day as the evening rolled into night, the bottled water had not yet arrived. Apparently some impatient kids and leaders didn't think brushing their teeth with the tap water was that big a deal ….

I remember the moaning. It was about 2 a.m.

It was coming from one of the leaders, big Charlie, and it was growing in intensity. Shortly after he started others began to faintly join in. "Oh, no ..." I thought, "this is going to be bad."

I can honestly say I have never heard anything like it. Big Charlie, with the suddenness of an NFL football player, shot to his feet, grabbed a large plastic garbage bag, and then just basically exploded. The sound was a horrid symphony of screaming, vomiting, and the sound of copious amounts of stomach contents pouring into the bag. Wow.

Do you know what sympathetic vomiting is?

The sound and smell of Charlie's episode triggered the whole room. Young men from every corner of the room began to join Charlie in what can only be described as a vomit-a-thon ... a twisted celebration of regurgitation. What made it even worse was that many of the teenage boys were not near as good as Charlie at finding a garbage bag.

Oh, the humanity ...

Roughly 35 of the 90 participants on the trip were swept up in this bacterial wrath. All because they couldn't hang on an extra hour for their bottled water. They paid dearly for their impatience.

Waiting is hard ... but it is often in our best interests. Especially when it comes to our relationship with God.

Faith and Waiting in the Bible

Forty-three times in the Old Testament alone, the people of God are commanded to wait on the LORD.

At the age of 75, Abraham is promised by God that he is going to father a child. Now at his age you would expect that the fulfillment of such a promise is imminent. But no ... Abraham would wait another 24 years before the miracle child Isaac is born.

Joseph would wait 20 years before his God-given dreams would come true.

The Hebrew people would wait, enduring 400 years of toil and slavery, before being delivered.

Moses would wait 40 years in the desert to finally bring deliverance to these people.

David would wait over a decade between his anointing as king, and his actual assumption of power.

Israel waited so long for its Messiah, that by the time Jesus arrived, only those whose eyes were especially fixed on it recognized him.

Jesus disciples impatiently badgered Jesus, "Lord will you restore the Kingdom now?" Waiting is hard.

Do you resonate with those disciples? Do you ever wish God moved more quickly? Author John Ortberg was right when he said, "We are double espresso followers of a decaf Sovereign." (I write this as I take a sip of my triple-shot white mocha.)

All kidding aside though – sometimes waiting can be excruciating – stretching our faith to its limits:

- The father of three boys waiting on a the test results of a biopsy

- The woman in her late thirties who waits on a life companion

- The political prisoner who waits for the world to notice injustice

- The faithful worker waiting for recognition and a promotion that never seems to come

I remember several years ago I drove to a rural town near where I live to visit a widowed elderly man named Ted. He was a tough old German, and conversation with him tended to be sparse. One day I just asked him, "Ted, how can I pray for you? What do you want?"

I'll never forget his answer.

"I miss my wife. I want to see her again. I'm tired of waiting. Pray that God will take me soon. I want to die."

The late Lewis Smedes, a teacher of mine at Fuller Seminary, once wrote,

> Waiting is our destiny as creatures who cannot by themselves
>   bring about what they hope for.
> We wait in darkness for a flame we cannot light,
> We wait in fear for a happy ending we cannot write.
> We wait for a not yet that feels like a not ever.
> Waiting is the hardest work of hope.[1]

Waiting is hard because we are human. Waiting is a work of hope because we wait on God. When I was young I was very impatient, but as I became a parent I began to understand aspects and angles of God's love in new and surprising ways. Perhaps the most notable aspect of God's love I have learned (and am still learning), is patience.

God Makes Us Wait to Protect Us

In America we live in a consumer culture designed to take advantage of our impulsivity. This is why the checkout lane at stores is lined with what are called "impulse items;" tabloid magazines, candy, soda pop, etc. These item are there because, strategically, that is where they sell best. Be honest, it probably wasn't that long ago when you were in one of those lines with all of your items on the belt, when out of the corner of your eye you saw that bag of M&Ms, and something in your brain said, "Oh what the heck … ."

One of the greatest lessons we can try to teach our kids is the biblical concept of delayed gratification. God instructs us to wait on certain things to protect us from the consequences of our own impulsive behavior.

He tells us to wait for sex until marriage, and yet our cultural landscape is littered with people hurting from broken relationships, sexually transmitted diseases, and fractured families because we couldn't.

God tells us to wait and resist rushing into debt, and yet our airwaves overflow with debt consolidation commercials.

---

1 | "Standing on the Promises."

Many of our Bible heroes suffered from the consequences of impulsivity:

- *Impatiently, Sarah convinces Abraham to father a child with her servant Hagar. The result would be conflict that continues even today.*[2]

- *Esau impulsively sells his birthright to Jacob for a bowl of stew.* [3]

- *Moses, seething with vengeful energy, kills an Egyptian in defense of his fellow Hebrew. The result would be 40 years of isolation in the desert before he would return to bring deliverance the right way.*[4]

- *Saul disobeys the LORD, and refuses to wait for Samuel to make sacrifice before a major battle. The result would be the slow but sure erosion of Saul's reign as king.*[5]

- *Simon the Sorcerer attempts to wield the gifts of the Holy Spirit without submitting to Jesus as his LORD first.*[6]

In his book *Emotional Intelligence*, psychologist Daniel Goleman makes the case that it is emotional quotient (EQ), not intelligence quotient (IQ),that is the biggest indicator of future life success and happiness. Among the most important traits, notes Goleman, is the ability to practice delayed gratification.

Goleman notes a now famous Stanford study in which 4-year-old children were given the choice to eat a marshmallow immediately, or wait a few minutes and get two marshmallows. These children were then tracked for many years. The results were that the kids who were able to delay gratification and wait for the two marshmallows, ended up much healthier later in life. In fact, the marshmallow waiters had SAT scores that were, on average, 210 points higher than the marshmallow grabbers!

God's desire to protect us from such impulsivity extends into the arena of our vocation and spiritual gifting, where impatience can

---

2 | Genesis 25
3 | Genesis 25
4 | Exodus 2
5 | 1 Samuel 13
6 | Acts 8

lead to stunted training, mixed motives, and immature decision making.

Education guru Parker Palmer tells the story of how being made to wait saved him from a bad vocational choice. Parker had been offered the position of president of a prestigious institution. With the position came a significant increase in pay, status and influence.

But Parker was a Quaker, and they have a tradition that vets out big decisions such as this through what is called a "clearness committee." The job of the clearness committee is not give advice, but to ask probing questions that would help Parker discern God's will in the matter. Parker would later confess that his original motive wasn't to discern God's will, but to brag to his friends about being offered a job he had already decided to accept.

John Ortberg relates from his book *If You Want to Walk On Water You Have to Get Out of the Boat*, how the meeting progressed:

> "For a while the questions were easy – what would Parker's vision be for this school; what mission would it serve in society, and so on. Then someone asked what appeared to be a very simple question: 'Parker, what would you like about being president?'

> "Oddly enough, Parker had to think about this one for a while. 'Well, I wouldn't like all the politics involved; I wouldn't like having to give up my study and teaching; I wouldn't like to have to raise funds. . . .'

> " 'Yes,' the questioner reminded him, 'but the question was what would you like?'

> " 'I'm coming to that,' he said irritably, then proceeded to list several more irksome things. 'I wouldn't like to have to give up my summer vacations, I wouldn't like. . .'

> "The question was called for a third time. Palmer writes,

> "I felt compelled to give the only honest answer I possessed, an answer that came from the very bottom of my barrel, an answer that appalled even me as I spoke it. 'Well,' said I, in the

smallest voice I possess, 'I guess what I'd like most is getting my picture in the paper with the word president under it.' I was sitting with seasoned Quakers who knew that though my answer was laughable, my mortal soul was clearly at stake! They did not laugh at all but went into a long and serious silence – a silence in which I could only sweat and inwardly groan.

"Finally my questioner broke the silence with a question that cracked all of us up – and cracked me open: 'Parker' he said, 'can you think of an easier way to get your picture in the paper?' "

God used the Quaker clearness committee to slow Parker down, and wait long enough to really consider his true motives. This group of men helped to save Parker from his own vocational impulsivity. He would have chosen the position for the wrong reasons. He would have chosen a vocation that didn't match his gifts.

Parker would go on to say, "You cannot choose your calling, you must let your life speak."

Sometimes waiting is a good thing.

God Makes Us Wait to Shape Us

We have times in our lives when we need to be reminded that God is the sculptor of our lives, and that we are the raw material – with all of its potential and limitations.

Businessman Michael Novak, in his book, *Business as a Calling*, says,

"We didn't give ourselves the personalities, talents, or longings we were born with. When we fulfill these – these gifts from beyond ourselves – it is like fulfilling something we were meant to do. . . . the Creator of all things knows the name of each of us – knows thoroughly, better than we do ourselves, what is in us, for he put it there and intends for us to do something with it – something that meshes with his intentions for many other people. . . . Even if we do not always think of it that way, each of us was given a calling – by fate, by chance, by destiny, by God. Those who are lucky have found it."

I think sometimes we forget that we are not finished products. We forget about our limitations and our immaturities, and thus our need for continuous refinement. This implies our constant need for humility, whether we embrace it willingly, or our limitations force it upon us. This is hard in an American culture that promotes the fallacy of what is called "the limitless self." This is the lie that we can accomplish any goal, pursue any vocation, and ascend to greatness if we just believe and never give up. As good as this sounds, it's a lie. Especially if it also doesn't take into account our raw material. Remember what we said about American Idol? Well, that is an excellent example of the illusion of the limitless self.

Sorry for continuing to bash you with Parker Palmer quotes, but he is just so good ... ☺

> "Like many middle-class Americans, especially those who are white and male, I was raised in a subculture that insisted I could do anything I wanted to, be anything I wanted to be, if I were willing to make the effort. The message was that both the universe and I were without limits, given enough energy and commitment on my part. God made things that way, and all I had to do was to get with the program.

> "My troubles began, of course, when I started to slam into my limitations, especially in the form of failure."

It might be safe to say that growth is the gift nobody wants. We want to be gifted, called, and used by God – but we want the shortcut – to skip the training.

Now, the training I am referring to here isn't necessarily formal education or the development of skill sets. I am talking about the character, strength, and perspective that are forged between the hammer of patience, and the anvil of our limitations.

Joseph had the raw material. He had the dream. He had his father's unfailing (if not somewhat dysfunctional) support. But as a young man what he probably didn't have was the moral fortitude to exercise his potential gifting and position to its fullest potential. God had more work to do with Joseph. And so Joseph would go to school. He would ...

- Attend the University of Betrayal (twice)
- Get his undergraduate degree in Slavery
- Do graduate work in Loss of Status
- Get a second degree in Prison Service
- Did his Doctoral Work in Humility Applications
- Graduated in Dream Interpretation (with a minor in Divine Credit Deflection)
- Found his calling in Nation Survival and Family Forgiveness
- Promoted to executive leadership (VP) specializing in Godly Perspective (demonstrated when he said to his betraying brothers, *"What you mean for evil God used for good"*)

You get my point.

Sometimes in the process of waiting, God shapes us in ways that lead us to gain new perspectives, prompting us to change direction or vocation. Henri Nouwen is just such a case study. Author Philip Yancey writes about Nouwen:

> *"Trained in Holland as a psychologist and a theologian, Nouwen spent his early years achieving. He taught at Notre Dame, Yale, and Harvard, averaged more than a book a year, and traveled widely as a conference speaker. He had a resume to die for – which was the problem, exactly. The pressing schedule and relentless competition were suffocating his own spiritual life.*

> *"Nouwen went to South America for six months, scouting a new role for himself as a missionary in the Third World. A hectic speaking schedule on his return to the United States only made things worse. Finally, Nouwen fell into the arms of the L'Arche community in France, a home for the seriously disabled. He felt so nourished by them that he agreed to become priest in residence at a similar home in Toronto called Daybreak. There, Nouwen spent his last ten years, still writing and traveling to speak here and there, but always returning to the haven of Daybreak."*[7]

---

7 | From an article Yancey wrote in Christianity Today entitled "The Holy Inefficiency of Henri Nouwen," December 9, 1996.

When, in the pursuit of our calling and gifts, should we stop pressing forward and wait on God? Once again, the answer has to do with learning to be at peace with our limitations as well as God's sovereignty.

God Makes Us Wait to Shape Our Circumstances
(Waiting makes us get out of God's way)

Some people are wired to take risk and press forward. Others are more risk averse and cautious. Neither is ultimately good or bad. It's just wiring. When considering whether you should move forward or wait upon God, one of the things that needs to be taken into account is which direction you tend to default toward. Remember, a big part of walking in God's calling is His character training. If you tend to be cautious, there is a good chance that God is going to find ways to spur you forward. If are like me and default towards moving, God is going to place you in situations that teach you patience.

God has been working on that patience thing in me my whole life …

I am a lot like the character Rudy from the movie of the same name. In the movie, Rudy has decided to pursue his dream of being on the Notre Dame football team. Given his raw material, it's a pretty audacious goal. He encounters resistance in all kinds of shapes and sizes; his jealous brother mocks him, his father discourages him, he struggles with academics due to dyslexia.

A priest at Notre Dame, Father Cavanaugh, gives Rudy a chance by getting him into the nearby junior college, Holy Cross. Rudy has to get good enough grades by the end of his second year to be accepted, or else his dream will be over. In a church, just before Rudy's last chance to transfer into Notre Dame, he has this conversation with Father Cavanaugh:

> **Father Cavanaugh:** *You did a hell of a job, kid, chasing down your dream.*
>
> **Rudy:** *I don't care what kind of job I did. If it doesn't produce any results, it doesn't mean anything.*

Father C: *I think you'll discover that it will.*

Rudy: *Maybe I haven't prayed enough.*

Father C: *I'm sure that's not the problem. Praying is something we do in our time. The answers come in God's time.*

Rudy: *Have I done everything I possibly can? Can you help me?*

Father C: *Son, in 35 years of religious studies, I've come up with only two hard incontrovertible facts: there is a God, and I'm not Him.*

The kindly priest gently encourages Rudy with the idea that no matter what news he ultimately gets, his efforts in the big picture will not be a waste. Rudy is so focused on his short-term goal, he is incapable of really understanding Father Cavanaugh's deeper point.

Rudy makes a common spiritual mistake:

We confuse the end of our efforts with the end of God's efforts.

It is possible that the end of our efforts really do signify the end. If that is true, we must learn to trust that God's "No" is for the best. I know this can be very hard. However, many times the end of our efforts actually constitutes the beginning of God's efforts. Sometimes God just flat out delights in getting us out of the way so He can display his power and glory. We have to be reminded, as Father Cavanaugh said, that there is a God, and *we are NOT Him.*

Biblically we see this principle at work in many places:

- Gideon is told to conquer 120,000 Midianites with a force of 300 men, using only pots, torches and trumpets. In faith, Gideon sits still and obeys little knowing that God's Spirit is fomenting irrational fear in the ranks of the enemy

- Saul is confronted by the risen Jesus on the road to Damascus. He is disabled to the point of being helpless. But even as he is taken into the city, Jesus is preparing a man named Ananias to receive him and pray for him.

- Cornelius, a God-fearing Roman Centurion, prays to the Jewish God but appears to get no response. What he doesn't know is that God is using dreams to break down Peter's prejudices in preparation for a visit. This visit will result in the salvation of Cornelius' whole family.

I have personally experienced this aspect of God's work many times throughout my life. However, one in particular stands out, and it has to do with how Pam and I ended attaining Providence Ranch.

About a year before finishing my seminary degree and getting ordained, I felt strongly that the time had come to explore with Pam one of her dreams.

Pam was one of those girls that had always loved horses. During her high school years, she had a horse name Dillion. Her parents boarded Dillion at a farm in south Bismarck. This allowed Pam to enjoy riding her horse on many beautiful afternoons across the rolling hills of the Missouri River bottoms. To this day we have a picture of her, at age 17, bounding with Dillion across the river. It is a rather poetic photo. But little did we know it would also be prophetic.

Our dream was bigger than merely purchasing and boarding a horse. I wanted her to have the lifestyle, and possibly make it an avenue for her own ministry calling. This would mean purchasing an equine property.

For two years we searched – hours and hours of calling, long country drives, open houses, and going to appointments. After a while a pattern emerged. If the property was a good one, we couldn't afford it. Conversely, if we could afford it – the property inevitably was a disaster. We explored buying land and building – but that was prohibitively expensive. Twice we found suitable, not perfect, but suitable properties and made an offer. The first owner didn't even bother to respond. The second couple, accepted our offer (yea!), but then pulled out one month into the process (ouch!). We were getting discouraged. More than once Pam wondered aloud if it just "wasn't meant to be."

Leaving no stones unturned (remember that principle?), I tried one last idea. Unbeknownst to Pam, I perused our list for the ten "dream" properties we would love to have, and then mailed a letter to each of them. *Keep in mind none of these places were for sale.* In the correspondence I explained who we were, what our dreams were (including doing ministry with the horses), and how their property could be a good fit. I included our contact information with the request that, should they decide to sell, we get first consideration to make an offer.

I know this was a pretty bold approach, but I was on my last stone.

Within a month, three of the ten property owners called me back, open to negotiating a sale. However, all of them took my letter for desperation, looking to make a deal well above market value.

Then it got quiet. No calls. No more searching. I was spent. I had turned over every stone I could think of.

One morning while driving, I cried out to God, "I give up. I don't know what else to do. God, if you want this to happen, you're going to have to do it – because I have failed." My heart broke for Pam.

Many months passed. And then it got weird – in a God kind of way.

Pam and I were at my parents on New Years Day 2005 when the phone rang. I was watching the Vikings lose (yet again) to the Redskins, but I couldn't help overhearing the conversation my mom was having.

"Oh hi …. Uh huh … yes I think they still are … uh huh … oh, that's OK … well, actually they are here, would you like to speak with Randy?"

The next thing I know I am on the phone with a lady named Darlene. She explained that they had received a letter from me a while back but set it aside. Things had changed for them recently and they wanted to know if we were still interested in a horse property.

Their property was the #1 property on my mailing list.

Within minutes, Pam and I were over there getting a tour. It was everything we had hoped for and more. A five acre parcel, complete with an A frame log home, horse barn, well and fencing. We had driven by this property many times and, with a disbelieving chuckle, fantasized about living at such a place. And now were sitting in it discussing a possible purchase. It was surreal.

The owner, a man named Don, who bore a striking resemblance to the actor Wilfred Brimley, interviewed us about what our intentions would be for a place like this – as if we were asking his daughter for her hand in marriage or something. In regards to a potential buyer, he clearly cared about the "who" and "why" part of the equation. After we shared our dream with them, he matter-of-factly asked us what we would pay for the property.

I felt trapped. The property was the nicest we had seen. Its market value was clearly way above our means. If I offered him what we could afford I feared it would be an insult.

"How about if you and Darlene discuss it and then call us when you feel you have a fair price?" I said.

He agreed. For a week we were on pins and needles whenever the phone rang. Pam and I prayed and prayed. I prayed very specifically. If this was the place, I needed to know God was in it. So I laid out a Gideon style fleece, and prayed for a price only God could be behind.

We continued to wait. Finally, about 10 days later, the call came. After a brief explanation of his logic, Don offered a sale price. It was significantly BELOW the number I was praying for! My stomach was doing cartwheels, but I tried to play it cool, "Well let me discuss it with Pam, and we'll get back to you."

I just sat there stunned for a minute. Then I told Pam. Then we just sat there stunned for a minute. It didn't seem possible, but there we were. Then we realized there was a problem. The price Don offered was too low. We reluctantly agreed that we couldn't accept it in good conscience. What do you do in such circumstances?

You go have pancakes.

A few days later our whole family met with Don and Darlene at the local Denny's. Don is not the "beat-around-the-bush" type and conversation quickly moved to the topic at hand.

"Don," I said firmly, "I understand why you arrived at the price you did, but Pam and I just don't feel it is acceptable."

Don's countenance shifted in preparation for negotiation.

I continued. "Pam and I discussed it, and we feel the price you are asking is too low. Your property is worth much more. We know, because we have seen what is out there. So ... what we would like to do is counter-offer at $5,000 higher. The truth is, you could probably get more than that, but that is our offer. We want this process to be fair to you and us."

Don tilted his head in surprise, a nervous smile crossing his face.

"Randy, I made a good living as a businessman, and I must say that what you have just told me makes no business sense whatsoever. Are you sure this is what you want to do?"

"Yes," I assured him. Though I wasn't a businessman, I felt a strong sense of peace and confidence about this course of action.

We finished our pancakes as he mulled over the unexpected developments. "I'll think about it. Give me 30 days."

"Of course" I agreed. Uhhh ... more waiting.

45 days later, I accidentally ran into him at the gas station. Surprised, he looked at me and smiled.

"I accept your offer. You can have the property. I'll have my attorney draw up the papers."

As he turned and left I quietly, and joyfully I peed my pants (OK – I mean that metaphorically – but you get my drift).

After doing everything we could possibly do, with no success, Pam and I had been reduced to helplessly waiting on a dream for which there seemed little hope. But the end of our efforts were only the beginning of God's efforts.

Seriously, how could this not be a God-thing? I mean everything about the process was wonderfully backwards:

- We attempted to buy a place that wasn't for sale.
- The owner contacted us after we had quit looking.
- The owner made the first offer – a price well below market.
- We counter-offered higher.

And the rest is history.

That is why we named it Providence Ranch.

When we had nothing left to give, God provided.

God wants to protect us.

He wants to grow us.

And sometimes He just smiles, gets us out of the way, and says, "Watch what I'm going to do."

Waiting is the hardest work of hope.
But, oh, what amazing work it is.

When To Wait On God

Mythbusters: Hesitations, Rationalizations, Procrastinations and Distractions

"We're going to have to let truth scream louder to our souls than the lies that have infected us."

– Beth Moore, *So Long, Insecurity: You've Been A Bad Friend To Us*

As of late, the books by pastor Tim Keller have been among my favorites. I love how he weaves scripture, history, philosophy, and even pop culture into his messages in ways that are easy to understand.[1] He is a very gifted individual.

OK – I'm jealous. But I'm jealous in all the right ways. ☺

In the introduction of his book, *Every Great Endeavor*, Tim recounts a little known nugget about JRR Tolkien. Tolkien is best known for his master works, *The Hobbit and The Lord of the Rings*. However, Tolkien also wrote many short stories for local publication. One such story was a delightful little tale entitled, "Leaf by Niggle." It was about a painter.

Tolkien chose the name "Niggle" for the painter intentionally. In the Oxford English Dictionary (of which Tolkien was a contributor), "niggle" was defined as *"to work ... in a fiddling or ineffective way ... to spend time unnecessarily on petty details."* This was Niggle. He was a perfectionist, always unhappy with what he had produced, often distracted, prone to worry and procrastination. We are also told in the story that Niggle "had a long journey to make." He did not want to go ... but he could not get out of it. This journey was symbolic of death.

Niggle had one picture in particular he wanted to paint before leaving on his journey. At first, in his mind's eye, it was just a leaf.

---

1 | Books I recommend are *The Reason for God*, *Every Good Endeavor*, and *The Prodigal God*. You can also listen to many of his sermons on YouTube.

But then he saw the whole tree, and then beyond that an entire vast landscape yawning behind it. It would require a canvas so large he would need a ladder to paint. This would be his goal – to finish this one work before departing.

Keller continues the story:

> "So he worked on his canvas, 'putting in a touch here, and rubbing out a patch there,' but he never got much done. There were two reasons for this. First, it was because he was the sort of painter who could paint leaves better than trees. He used to spend a long time on a single leaf,' ... the second reason was his 'kind heart.' Niggle was constantly distracted by doing things his neighbors asked him to do for them ...

> "Eventually, the time for Niggle's 'journey' arrived, though he was not done with his masterpiece. Realizing he must go, Niggle bursts into tears of regret and failure. Sometime after his death, his incomplete painting is discovered and hung in the recess of the town museum. Very few eyes notice it. Entitled 'Leaf by Niggle,' it features only one beautiful leaf."

How many of us can relate to Niggle? We struggle with our personal forms of hesitations, procrastinations, rationalizations, and distractions. We fix goals in our hearts, telling ourselves "This one thing – this I will accomplish," only to often be derailed and disappointed.

And so as I begin this chapter, I want to affirm our common identity in Niggle. We all struggle with habits and mindsets that hold us back. As we explore the most common of these gift-crippling myths, I want to reassure you that my intention is not to scold, mock or condemn. Rather it is to say, "I know ... I understand ... I've been there ... now let's move forward."

Don't lose heart. There is much learning to be done. And I also suspect that we aren't yet done with the story of Niggle – because with God, there is always another page in the chapter!

Myth #1 - Hesitations: "What If I Choose the Wrong Path?"

One of the most common phrases meant to encourage people in discipleship is "God loves you and has an amazing plan for your life."

What I have found, however, is that for some people, the thought of God having a plan for their lives is terrifying. This isn't because they don't want a plan, it's because they are frozen by the fear that they might miss it.

"Here's the plan I made for your life," they hear God saying in their head, "Don't miss it – don't screw it up."

They are afraid that in the end, instead of hearing, "Well done, good and faithful servant," they are going to hear, "Is that the best you could do?"

This myth, this false mindset is rooted in an overly rigid understanding of how God's will functions. They are too focused on the specific path, and not focused enough on the destination. I'm not saying the path doesn't matter, what I'm saying is it is possible to put too much emphasis on the path, and not enough on God as your navigator.

God – as navigator? Yes. God doesn't just throw us in the car with a huge, crumpled up map and say, *"See you there – I hope."* (That would be terrifying.) No – God is there alongside for the duration of the trip, ready to give correction whenever a wrong turn is taken, or an obstacle forces a new course.

And that's the beauty of it – with God alongside you for the journey, many courses are possible to the same destination.

"Re-computing." What a comforting word. Even as I write this book I am doing while on retreat in Pasadena CA. I am not native to the Los Angeles area – thus you could imagine that getting around could be a complete nightmare. But it's not. Why? Because today we have navigation apps in our cars and phones. Last year I decided to drive to Santa Monica Pier and up the coastal highway. After entering my destination into my phone navigation app, the voice gave me step-by-step instructions on exactly how

to get there. However, about 20 minutes into the journey, road construction forced me to bypass an exit I was supposed to take. When that happens in the place the size of LA, your heart skips a beat. But then I heard it ...

"Re-computing."

Instantly, my knuckles relaxed their grip on the steering wheel. The app was going to find a new path to the destination – no problem, I just needed to trust the directions and keep going.

God works this way. This is why He desires day-to-day relationship with us more than anything else. He has a destination in mind for each of us, but within that sovereign will, many courses are possible.

Make a mistake?	*"Re-computing."*
Make a wrong choice?	*"Re-computing."*
Get lost?	*"Re-computing."*

What is probably most amazing about this dynamic is that even when we intentionally go off course through sin and rebellion, God is still there offering redirection – if only we would listen and turn around. He will not force us to change course – but He is always there to re-direct our steps when we are ready.

"Thy word is a lamp unto my feet, and a light unto my path."[2]

" ... if we are faithless, He remains faithful, for He cannot deny Himself."[3]

Think of the characters from scripture that experienced this:

Adam and Eve ate the forbidden fruit – *"Re-computing"*

Abraham impatiently fathered Ishmael - *"Re-computing"*

David commits adultery, and then murder - *"Re-computing"*

Jonah runs from God's command - *"Re-computing"*

Saul of Tarsus persecutes the early church - *"Re-computing"*

---

2 | Psalm 119:5
3 | 2 Timothy 2:13

God is not just riding shotgun with us – He is our navigator. If we trust that, we need not fear getting off course as we move forward.

Myth #2 - Rationalizations: "What If I'm Too Young?"

No. You're not too young.

You may lack experience, knowledge, education, some character training, etc. But that is never an excuse not to move forward with God in service. The word "young" is simply not allowed to be synonymous with the aforementioned things.

> " 'In the last days,' God says, 'I will pour out my Spirit on all people. Your sons and daughters will prophesy, your young men will see visions, your old men will dream dreams.' "[4]

> "Therefore I remind you to stir up the gift of God which is in you through the laying on of my hands. For God has not given us a spirit of fear, but of power and of love and of a sound mind."[5]

It is simply not up to us who God decides to use, and at what stage of life. Experience, knowledge, wisdom … these are all important, but they are secondary to a heart that seeks after God. Joseph, Gideon, King David, King Solomon, David, Esther, the disciple John, Timothy; these were not people who stumbled ass-backwards into their callings. No, they were chosen by God, called by God, guided by God, and equipped by God.

Education, experience, wisdom are things that you gain as you walk with God, they are not pre-requisites to starting.

The process of walking with God is not a neat, clean process. In fact, it is messy by design. Discovering and nurturing your spiritual gifts puts us into situations whereby we learn the heart of God through love. In his book, Messy Spirituality, Mike Yaconelli relates a story by Doug Webster[6] about an idealistic college student who learned the messy beauty of this truth:

---

4 | Acts 2:17
5 | These are the words of Paul written to young Timothy in 2 Timothy 1:6-7.
6 | From his book "The Easy Yoke."

"A brand new Christian, this wide-eyed urban missionary didn't have a clue how to evangelize the inner city (Philadelphia). Frightened and anxious to share his new faith, the young man approached a very large tenement house. Cautiously making his way through the dark, cluttered hallways, he gingerly climbed up one flight of stairs to an apartment. He knocked on the door, and a woman holding a naked, howling baby opened it. She was smoking a not in any mood to hear some white, idealistic college boy tell her about Jesus. She started cursing him and slammed the door in his face. The young man was devasted.

"He walked out to the street, sat on the curb, and wept. "Look at me. How in the world could someone like me think I could tell anyone about Jesus?" Then he remembered that the baby was naked and the woman was smoking. The plan forming in his head didn't seem terribly spiritual, but ...

"He ran down the street to the local market and bought box of diapers and a pack of cigarettes. When he knocked on the door again, he showed the woman his purchases. She hesitated and then invited him in. For the rest of the day, he played with the baby and changed its diapers (even though he had never changed diapers before). When the woman offered him a cigarette, even though he didn't smoke, he smoked. He spent the entire day smoking and changing diapers. Never said a word about Jesus. Late in the afternoon, the woman asked him why he was doing all this, and finally he got to tell her everything he knew about Jesus. Took him five minutes. When he stopped talking, the woman looked at him and said softly, 'Pray for me and my baby that we can make it out of here alive,' so he did."[7]

For young people, the journey of discovering spiritual giftedness often starts with mission trips, and diverse ways to serve needs.

I recently read how a young teen at our local high school helped to entrepreneurially started a program to bring more friendships and community to the mentally disabled at their school. This person made arrangements for other students to befriend and accompany the disabled students to sporting events, concerts,

---

7 | By the way, if all you are thinking about after reading this is that this young man smoked cigarettes, then you are missing the point.

homework study sessions, and even just table company during school lunch periods. I cannot say for sure this was motivated specifically by Christian love, but I have my suspicions …☺[8]

Myth #3: What If I'm Too Easily Distracted?

The Bible talks about the fruits of the Spirit; love, joy, peace, patience, kindness, goodness, faithfulness, gentleness and self-control.[9]

To be sure, these are all very good and desirable traits. As we walk with God the fruits of the Spirit will emerge and grow. But let's be honest, in today's world it is a challenge to patiently nurture these traits when we are *literally being conditioned for distraction.* Our attention spans are being shaped every time we watch TV or view Internet content.

You doubt me? Consider the following:

In the early days of print media, the text portion of advertisements used to dominate the page. Here is the text from a 1905 Coca-Cola ad:

"Coca-Cola is a delightful, healthful and palatable beverage. It relieves fatigue and is indispensable for business and professional men, students, wheelman, and athletes. It relieves mental and physical exhaustion and is the favorite drink for ladies when thirsty, weary, and despondent. Coca-Cola, the most refreshing drink in the world."

Compare that to the text in an ad today:

"Coca-Cola: Open happiness."

This phenomenon is even more prevalent in television advertising. The same ad that would run one full minute during Ed Sullivan's show, then would run 30 seconds during the Johnny Carson era,

---

8 | See "Mentor Program Aims to Make Century More Inclusive," Bismarck
    Tribune, Feb. 20, 2016
9 | Galatians 5:22-23

now runs no longer than 15 seconds today. In fact, more and more ads are in the 10-second range.[10]

We are daily being trained for short attention spans, and often don't even realize it. I remember going to my grandmas when I was a kid to visit. Would you believe it actually took almost 15 minutes for her to brew coffee? Today, if I don't get my triple shot, non-fat skinny vanilla latte in less than two minutes I get ... well ... edgy.

Anyone relate?

A high school girl named Emily Mueller shares her struggle with meeting the demands of what a traditional Christian is supposed to look and act like within the challenges of ADHD:

> "I've often wondered how my ADHD fits into my life as a Christian. So many of the characteristics of my ADHD simply aren't conducive to the stereotypical model of what a Christian woman should look like. I'm not quiet; I'm actually pretty loud. I can't sit still through prayer – even if it's 30 seconds, if I'm not the one speaking, my mind wanders. I'd much rather get up and move around than sit and listen to someone talk. I'm easily distracted, easily excitable, and am far more prone to fluctuations of emotion of epic proportions than a quiet spirit."[11]

I feel for Emily. But even more, at a certain level I empathize with her.

Is there any hope? Yes, I believe so. Part of what we need to understand is that we are who we are, and then explore how we can let God work through our fallen identity in ways that still please him. Yes, I understand we need to embrace the transformation that comes with the Holy Spirit. But we also need to start somewhere.

Part of the problem involves the traditional stereotype of what a Christian is supposed to conform to.

---

10 | This is why you often now see product placement in actual TV shows or movies. Corporations need to find new ways to get their product in front of your eyes to make up for the short attention spans they helped create.

11 | From Emily's blog the "ADHD Christian," Feb. 7, 2010.

- Christians are supposed to do "quiet time" everyday, sitting still, reading the word and praying a 5-point prayer for 30 minutes.

- Christians are supposed to be excited about sitting down for 2 hour sessions of intercessory prayer.

- Christians are supposed to love being in 1-hour board meetings that regularly run 3 hours.

- Christians are supposed to love 45-minute, 3-point sermons, and when they go long – yell for more.

Folks – can I be honest?
I struggle with every one of those examples – and I'm a pastor.

I don't necessarily feel the presence of God doing a traditional devotional time. But I do feel God's presence powerfully when I'm running and listening to music (I feel like some of my most significant times of prayer and confession have occurred in the middle of a 5-mile run).

I would rather light my hair on fire than go to a two-hour intercessory prayer meeting. Sorry – just being honest. But let me fire off prayers while I'm going about the course of my day – or in response to some personal counseling with a hurting person – and I'm there.

Am I mocking the traditional approaches listed above? No not at all. I know they really work for many people – and I appreciate that. I also understand deeply the power of employing the spiritual disciplines. I just think this there is more than one way of practicing them. I don't want people like Emily to feel like second-class citizens because they are wired differently. Allowing us different ways to express and experience our relationship with Jesus enhances the body of Christ.

It's important to have some biblical perspective when considering this myth. God uses an amazing diversity of different people. Being different does not disqualify you, nor should it ever be an excuse to shirk your calling.

The prophets of the Old Testament were different. To say that they were creative in communicating the Word of the LORD would be an understatement. They definitely didn't fit the mold. Imagine if your pastor did in church some of the things these guys did before kings. Journalist Stephen Beale recounts them:

> "Consider Isaiah, who stripped off all his clothes and wandered around naked (Isaiah 20).
>
> "Or Jeremiah, who not only hid his underwear in a rock but then went back to retrieve it after a 'long time' (Jeremiah 13). Jeremiah apparently didn't mind parting with under-garments, but he couldn't be separated from the cattle yoke he had fastened to his shoulders until another prophet broke it off (Jeremiah 27 and 28).
>
> "Yet another eyebrow-raiser was Hosea, who married a prostitute and named their daughter Lo-ruhama, which means 'unloved' (Hosea 1).
>
> "Then there was Jonah, the run-away prophet who spent three days in the belly of a whale before answering God's call.
>
> "The weirdest of the lot may be Ezekiel. After witnessing a vision of God flanked by four chimerical creatures, the prophet ate a scroll that had been given to him (Ezekiel 1 and 3). Ezekiel was called to be a prophet, but his ministry initially did not involve any prophetic words, as God had rendered him mute (Ezekiel 3). Instead he took to drawing, depicting an image of Jerusalem under siege on a clay tablet. Then he lay down on his side, with an iron pan separating him from his clay art. After 390 days had passed, Ezekiel rolled over and repeated (Ezekiel 4).
>
> "After his clay tablet stunt was over, Ezekiel went on a new diet of barley cakes baked over cow manure (Ezekiel 4). Next Ezekiel used a sword – yes, you read that right, an actual sword – to shave off his beard, dividing his hairs into thirds. He set one third on fire. He scattered another third around the city and stabbed it with his sword. He threw the remaining third into the wind. But the hair histrionics were far from over: Ezekiel had saved a few hairs from such abuse, which he sewed into his clothing. Then he burned some of those hairs too (Ezekiel 5)."

Oh, by the way, Mr. Beale then reminds us one very important point:

> One crucial detail has been omitted in these accounts: the actions of Ezekiel, Hosea, Jeremiah, and Isaiah were commanded by God, which means that we cannot dismiss their behavior. **Indeed, these men were not prophets in spite of their eccentricities. Rather, their actions were at the center of their ministry.**[12]

The truth, I believe, is that the body of Christ needs people who are more able to move spontaneously and creatively. I believe that for every structured administrator, the church needs two off-the-wall prophets.

Why?
Because relationships matter even more than "getting things done."

I have a friend named Ernie. Though he is in his 50's, only recently has he been formally diagnosed with ADHD. To be sure, Ernie is not the guy you want organizing and structuring traditional church ministries or by-laws. But I must tell you, when we are out and about the town together, I am stunned and humbled by his ability to relate with people – especially people he doesn't know! While I am being merely polite, Ernie is engaging these people in ways that light them up and make their day. As I watch him in all his holy frivolity, I find myself drawn in – and in the process sense the love of Jesus in ways that go beyond everyday ministry.

I am thankful to have Ernie in my life. He teaches me about the love of Jesus in ways that are infectious – not in spite of his distracted nature, but because of it.

Myth #4: "What If I'm Too Old?"
(Subtitle: God Loves Late Bloomers)

This final section is important to me. In an American culture that not only values, but worships youth, it is easy for seasoned citizens to think that discussions about calling and giftedness are a "young person's" game.

---

12 | "The Crazy Prophets," The Catholic Exchange, Nov.18, 2013.

Nothing could be further from the truth.
For the American worker, retirement is a goal.
For the follower of Jesus, there is no such thing as retirement.

Nearing his mid 60's, our former Sr. Pastor, Bob Nordvall, was the perfect example of how a Christian (not just pastors) should approach the next stage. He didn't see his retirement from the pastoral ministry as the end of his working years. Rather he saw it as new stage of his working years. He was fond of saying that he wasn't going to retire – **but refire!**

After 25 years of ministry, I can totally understand where he is coming from. I can certainly see that at some point I will move on from the pastoral ministry. But at no point – at least until my body gives up – can I see myself not doing some kind of ministry. I have no idea what God has in store for me at the next stage – but as far as I'm concerned – I'm locked into a lifetime contract for Kingdom work.

You are never too old for God's calling.

Let's take a second look at Acts Chapter 2:

> "In the last days, God says,
> I will pour out my Spirit on all people.
> Your sons and daughters will prophesy,
> your young men will see visions,
> **your old men will dream dreams."**

Notice it doesn't say, "your old men will occupy rocking chairs," or "your old women will binge watch episodes of Days of Our Lives."

No – God's calling is never rescinded. There is too much at stake. For some people, that means continuing on a path already established. For others, it opens up the possibility of new experiences and adventures. It represents the chance to explore fresh passions, hopes and dreams in the name of the Kingdom – maybe even for the first time.

God loves late bloomers.

For some, late blooming might happen within the scope of their vocation.

- C.S. Lewis did his most significant writing the last 20 years of his life.

- Alexander Fleming didn't receive the Nobel Prize for his discovery of Penicillin until age 64.

- Jockey Calvin Borel raced horses for forty years, but won no races of any significance until the final ten years of his career. Borel won the Kentucky Derby in 2007, 2009 and 2010, as well as the Preakness in 2009.

For others, late blooming entails the flowering of entirely new vocations at an age when most people stop working.

- Harlan Sanders, after careers as a steam engine stoker, insurance salesman, and filling station operator, didn't franchise his first Kentucky Fried Chicken restaurant until he was 62.

- Grandma Moses didn't take up painting until age 80.

- Laura Wilder (*Little House on the Prairie*) and Wilbert Awdry (*Thomas the Tank Engine*) didn't take up writing careers until later in life.

Of course, the Bible is full of late bloomers.

- Noah gathers the largest floating zoo in history at age 600

- Sarah gives birth to Isaac in her late 90's (without the epidural)

- Moses is called to bring deliverance for the Hebrews at age 80

- Zacharius doesn't see the promised Messiah until his life's end

- Nicodemus and Joseph of Arimathea come to know God at the end of their careers – despite opposition from their colleagues.

As we grow older it is easy to begin to think we are outdated, outmoded, out of touch, and thus ... outsiders. Don't believe it. Don't give in to it. Keep growing, keep serving, and keep learning.

You can start today by taking the survey in this book. Who knows – you just might discover new dreams and opportunities God has hidden inside you for such a season of life as this.

Which brings me back to Tolkien's parable about Niggle.

It turns out that Niggle's death wasn't the end of the story. While the people in town went on with life, occasionally noticing his painting of the leaf in the town museum, God was at work in realms unseen.

Again, I'll let Tim Keller tell it.

> "After death Niggle is put on a train toward the mountains of the heavenly afterlife. At one point on his trip he hears two Voices. One seems to be Justice, the severe voice, which says Niggle wasted so much time and accomplished so little in life. But the other, gentler voice ('though it was not soft'), which seems to be Mercy, counters that Niggle has chosen to sacrifice for others, knowing what he was doing.

> "As a reward, when Niggle gets to the outskirts of the heavenly country, something catches his eye. He runs to it – and there it is: Before him stood the Tree, his Tree, finished; its leaves opening, its branches growing and bending in the wind that Niggle had so often felt or guessed, and yet had so often failed to catch. He gazed at the Tree, and slowly he lifted his arms and opened them wide. 'It is a gift!' he said."

> "The world before death – his old country – had forgotten Niggle almost completely, and there his work had ended unfinished and helpful to only a very few. But in his new country, the permanently real world, he finds that his tree, in full detail and finished, was not just a fancy of his that had died with him. No, it was indeed part of the True Reality that would live and be enjoyed forever."

Tolkien is writing about himself. Tolkien is Niggle. His preparation for writing The *Lord of the Rings* happened just as World War II was aflame. With daily air raid sirens blaring, and Nazi invasion a real possibility, Tolkien despaired that he might never get his masterpiece, his 'Tree' finished. For a time this despair held a death grip on his creativity.

But Tolkien, with help from his friend C.S. Lewis, found comfort in the story of Niggle, and eventually he found the momentum to work again. Drawing from his Christian understanding of vocation, Tolkien came to rest in the mysterious truth that every gift, talent and effort offered in the name of Christ, no matter how incomplete it might appear, would have lasting impact.

Our imperfect efforts, in the hands of a perfect God, can change the world, both now and forever.

Tolkien had readied himself, through Christian truth, for very modest accomplishment in the eyes of this world. Of course, the sweet irony is he eventually produced a work of genius that many today consider one the greatest literary works of history.

The Apostle Paul, another late bloomer, wrote:

"In the Lord, your labor is not in vain."[13]

You're never too old, too young, or too distracted for God. Let the great Navigator steer your course … and fear not.

"Re-computing."

---

13 | 1 Corinthians 15:58

Understanding The Supernatural Gifts

"It is never a question of how much you and I have of the Spirit, but how much He has of us."

Billy Graham

In the last chapter, I shared how music seems to help usher me into the presence of God – or a sense of connectedness with him. I can't explain how or why exactly – but I do know there is something about music that seems to awaken and sharpen my spiritual antennae.

The beauty, grandeur and delicacy of nature also have this effect on me. In my previous book, *The End is the Beginning*, I allude to what the Celts called "thin places" – places where the space between heaven and earth is very narrow – places where you can be unexpectedly taken up into a reality more ancient, deep and real.[1] These places and moments come and go as they please, and are resistant to any attempt to create them or make them happen. They are glimpses of mystery, signs of a future destiny that must be appreciated, but not clung to.

C.S. Lewis used the German word *sehnsucht* (meaning 'deep longings') to describe such moments ....

> *"... they are only the scent of a flower we have not found, the echo of a tune we have not heard, news from a country we have never yet visited."*[2]

These moments haunted Lewis during his childhood and early adult life. An avowed skeptic and atheist, Lewis couldn't intellectually shake the feeling that moments of sehnsucht weren't just renegade feelings, but rather hints and whispers of something trying to communicate with him – someone trying to reveal himself to him. At the encouragement of his good friend Owen Barfield, Lewis started reading authors George McDonald

---

1 | Chapter 18
2 | *The Weight of Glory*, p.45.

and G.K. Chesterton, and for the first time in his life, found ideas which unapologetically and powerfully married solid logic with a sense of the mysterious. Both authors were Christians. Lewis would later write that, one night while reading Chesterton's *The Everlasting Man*, he could feel the God he had so long resisted closing in on him,

> "You must picture me," Lewis wrote, "alone in that room in Magdalen (college), night after night, feeling, whenever my mind lifted even for a second from my work, the steady, unrelenting approach of Him whom I so earnestly desired not to meet."[3]

The conversion of C.S. Lewis was undoubtedly a product of irrefutable truth and irresistible mystery. The experiences of *sehnsucht* he could not resist were later affirmed by rational and biblical truth he could not deny. He would later go on to say,

> "I believe in Christianity as I believe that the sun has risen. Not only because I see it, but because by it I see everything else."

When God wants to reveal himself, there's no stopping him. But it is rarely a revelation of overwhelming power. More often God haunts, whispers, and nudges – revealing his mind and heart in small doses. This is because God desires for us to fall in love with him, not submit to him only in awe.

I believe that every person has within them a hunger for the mysterious – an antenna just waiting to awaken and receive signal from the divine.

Think for a moment ... have you had moments of *sehnsucht*? Do you have a 'thin place' where you sense there is something greater and more beautiful? Have you ever gazed upon an ocean sunset, a mountain vista, or a prairie thunderstorm and thought, "This can't be an accident"? Have you ever listened to some music and found your heart moved and swept up in surprising ways?

We are wired for mystery. Logic and rational thought are gifts of God, and marvelous tools, but they don't feed our souls – do they?

---

3 | From Lewis' autobiography *Surprised By Joy*, p.228.

We don't experience life as a math problem – we experience it as a story.[4]

And so I begin this chapter on the supernatural gifts with these thoughts because the first thing I want to emphasize is that *spiritual gifts which are mysterious in nature* should be embraced – even if they are not fully understood. There is no denying it – we were made for mystery.

Coming Clean About the Supernatural Gifts

For the remainder of this chapter I am basically going to tell two stories.

Both involve my personal experience with the supernatural gifts. One story will reflect a more negative experience, the other a more positive experience. As I walk through each with you, it is my intention to come clean about my specific thoughts and conclusions on how these gifts are to be experienced, practiced and managed in the church. So as not to leave you trying to read between the lines, here are the points I want to make:

- The supernatural gifts are real and present in the church today.

- The supernatural gifts should be embraced but managed carefully.

- No gift, including any of the supernatural gifts, is for everybody.

- Some gifts are more public than others, but all are equal in importance.

- Tongues is not an exclusive indicator of genuine Christian faith.

- All spiritual gifts can be misused or abused.

- The supernatural gifts have often been a source of division.

- God works through the gifts even when people mess it up.

---

4 | See John Eldredge's wonderful little book *Epic* for on these thoughts.

The Supernatural Gifts:
The Experience of a Naïve Lutheran

I was raised a Lutheran, and went through the classic Lutheran training regimen – infant baptism, first Bible, First Communion, Confirmation. I even preached on "Youth Sunday" – which I think was our church's way of assuaging its guilt over a non-existent youth ministry. I graduated knowing the right stuff – but lacking a living relationship with Jesus Christ.[5]

During my college years, I walked through a wilderness period, embracing the role of the prodigal son. I didn't outright reject my Christian upbringing, I still wanted Jesus for fire insurance, but the only Lord I was willing to follow was myself. After about five years of this subconscious arrangement, it was painfully obvious to me that my life was a mess.

Turns out I wasn't a very good God.

As I was finishing my undergraduate work at Moorhead State University, I began to go through a spiritual re-awakening. Unlike high school, at college I had some friends who were pretty devout believers. They weren't crazy or obnoxious, but the conviction of their beliefs did make them stand out among the typical college crowd. Without my realizing it, they were nurturing me back into the faith. They were Pentecostals. I didn't know what a Pentecostal was. I was about to find out….

One night they invited me to church. It had been a long time since I went to church. I was spiritually hungry again and looked forward to it. The name on the outside said "Assemblies of God" and the sanctuary was bigger than at my church. The music was different too – more modern. It was a pleasantly startling experience – the people around me were … well, for lack of a better word … singing. Loudly. Passionately. (Garrison Keillor would tell you the Lutheran's have the market cornered on singing … but compared to what I heard, Lutheran singing was more like mumbling in four-part harmony).

---

5 | I want to emphasize that this was not the fault of my Pastor, Jay Stratton, or my parents. I was my own agent – though it didn't help that I had virtually no friends or classmates who had an alive faith (except for my friend Jay Heinz, and girlfriend and future wife Pam).

The pastor got up to preach. Wow. It was good. I could actually follow him. He was preaching specifically from the Bible – what I later learned to be "expository preaching." I still remember the text to this day: 1 Corinthians 18-25 – *"for the foolishness of God is greater than the wisdom of this world."*

At the close of the service, the pastor invited anybody who wanted to be filled with the Holy Spirit to come forward for prayer. I remember when I was confirmed there was a prayer for the Holy Spirit. "Sounds good to me," I thought to myself. At that stage of my life, I would take all the help I could get. So I went forward expecting a nice short prayer, followed by fish and chips at Skipper's. Oh boy ...

At first the prayer was fine – comforting, encouraging, earnest. But after about five minutes, it became clear to me that they were expecting something to happen. "Just let it go," someone said. Let what go? I was supposed to do something – but I had no idea what. Another couple of minutes went by, and the group started interpreting my confusion with resistance. Then someone said, "Let's take this one to the back room."

What started out as comforting and encouraging got scary. "What did I get myself into ..." I thought, desperately, now scanning the room for an escape route.

"Let it go, just let it go ... just trust the Holy Spirit and open your mouth," said the ring-leader (he no longer felt like a prayer partner to me).

Finally, I confessed to the men that I had no idea what they wanted. As they explained the spiritual gift of speaking in tongues, and read from the book of Acts, I experienced a strange collision of emotions. On the one hand, if there really was a way to experience God mysteriously, then I wanted it – as long as it was authentic. And that's where the rub was.

Even after the explanation and continued prayer, the expected manifestation wasn't happening. It's not that I was resisting – it's just that speaking in tongues wasn't happening. "Just say whatever comes out of your mouth," someone said with a stressful hint of annoyance. The pressure by this point was immense. I got the feeling that if I didn't say something, I wasn't going to go anywhere.

So I did it. I gave in. I mumbled something. It was cheating, but I needed to get out of that room. The animated response from the group encouraged me, so I mumbled it again a little louder. Shouts of "Thank you, Lord" and "Praise God" filled the room. Finally, after about 20 minutes, I was free.

I was confused. I wanted a real experience with the Holy Spirit, but I felt violated. My friends encouraged me saying, "Good for you, you got your prayer language!" They explained to me that I was to use this new language (mumbling) in my prayer time from that point on. "OK," I thought, "Maybe I'm supposed to try."

For two weeks after I prayed in that "language" every night. I tried to be as authentic as I could. I prayed aloud mixing English in with the "tongues." Finally, after about 20 minutes of prayer one night, I just stopped. I looked to up to God, feeling defeated, and cried out, "This doesn't feel real, God. I want to know you. I want your Holy Spirit. But I don't want to fake it. I want it to be real. I think you want it to be real too." Then it got quiet. I didn't say anything. I didn't try to work at my prayer language. I just sat there. Nobody said anything. Not me. Not God. It felt good to rest. And then ... *sehnsucht*.

A tingle ran up my spine. I didn't see anything or hear anything. I just felt like I was being embraced. In the stillness and quiet God was there – with no fanfare whatsoever. That felt real. I sensed the Holy Spirit saying to me, "Quit trying. I got this. I was there in the church. I did fill you. I did give you a gift. Be patient. In time you will see ..."

That night I made a deal with God. It went like this: I would be always be open to Him, gifting me however he wanted. But ... if He was going to gift me supernaturally, He would have to knock me out. It would have to be so overwhelming and obvious that I would know without a doubt it was Him.

Fourteen years later, He would make good on that deal.

But wait ... let's process this story.

The Wizard of Oz Effect

So, was my experience in the church that night fraudulent? No, it wasn't.

After nearly 30 years of reflection, this is what I would say it was:

It was an imperfect church, praying in an imperfect way, for an imperfect person, in the name of a perfect God. This has been the way of the church from its inception – messy ministry that somehow God still uses for his glory.

In a roundabout way I call this the Wizard of Oz Effect. The wizard isn't quite who he is supposed to be, but despite that, the gifts sought by Dorothy's party (Lion – courage, Tin Man – heart, Scarecrow – brain) still emerge. Good things still happen.

Likewise, the church is not always what it's supposed to be (obviously), and yet in the mess of ministry, God still does amazing works and gives amazing gifts.

I don't believe my presence in the church that night was a mistake. God was going to do something in my life that night. It was just going to be messy.

Messy, because the people praying for me mistakenly believed that all true believers should manifest the gift of tongues. Yes, I know my Pentecostal friends will disagree with me. That's OK. We will agree to disagree. But it seems clear to me from scripture that speaking in tongues was not intended to be a universal gift. Addressing the Corinthian church about this issue, Paul stresses that the purpose of the spiritual gifts are for service, not status. The diversity of gifts was to be reflected in the diversity of believers, so that the body might be interdependent in its love for each other, and united in its proclamation of the Gospel. In making this point, Paul seeks to correct those in the church who have gotten caught up in thinking that everybody should have certain gifts (tongues), and that some gifts (those which are supernatural) are more important than others. He drives it home with a series of rhetorical questions that clear up the matter:

> "But God has put the body together, giving greater honor to the parts that lacked it, so that there should be no division in

the body, but that its parts should have equal concern for each other. If one part suffers, every part suffers with it; if one part is honored, every part rejoices with it."

*"Now you are the body of Christ, and each one of you is a part of it. And God has placed in the church first of all apostles, second prophets, third teachers, then miracles, then gifts of healing, of helping, of guidance, and of different kinds of tongues. **Are all apostles? Are all prophets? Are all teachers? Do all work miracles? Do all have gifts of healing? Do all speak in tongues? Do all interpret?** Now eagerly desire the greater gifts."[6]*

The answer to each of these concluding rhetorical questions is, of course, "No." Are all apostles? No. Are all prophets? No. Are all teachers? No. Do all work miracles? No. Do all have gifts of healing? No. Do all speak in tongues? No. Do all interpret? No.

Notice that Paul specifically applies these rhetorical questions to the gifts that people tend to mistakenly elevate, and these include the supernatural gifts; prophecy, teaching, miracle working, healing, tongues and interpretation.

It amazes me that we still get this wrong today. However, this does NOT mean that tongues and the other supernatural gifts should be eliminated from the church either. Paul is clear that the gifts of tongues, prophecy and interpretation have their place in worship.

"Follow the way of love and eagerly desire gifts of the Spirit, especially prophecy. For anyone who speaks in a tongue does not speak to people but to God. Indeed, no one understands them; they utter mysteries by the Spirit. But the one who prophesies speaks to people for their strengthening, encouraging and comfort. Anyone who speaks in a tongue edifies themselves, but the one who prophesies edifies the church. I would like every one of you to speak in tongues, but I would rather have you prophesy. The one who prophesies is greater than the one who speaks in tongues, unless someone interprets, so that the church may be edified ...

---

6 | 1 Corinthians 12

"Therefore, my brothers and sisters, be eager to prophesy, and do not forbid speaking in tongues. But everything should be done in a fitting and orderly way."[7]

So ... I did not receive the gift of tongues that night. Does that mean I wasn't filled with the Holy Spirit or didn't receive any gift? Again, I would say no. I do believe I received the Holy Spirit and his gifting that night, it's just that God had a longer term plan to work out. I needed some time to struggle and grow. I needed time to follow some dreams that ultimately would not serve as destinations, but as byways leading to my more God-given calling.

As I wrestled with God over my vocation, I realized it was likely coming down to a showdown over what I wanted verses what God wanted. I remember one night, on warm night in Nashville, TN, this wanna-be music producer prayed one of the scariest, and yet empowering prayers a person could ever pray ... "God, if I never write or play another note of music again, but what I do pleases you – then let it be so."

Really, it was just my own version of Jesus words, "Seek first the Kingdom of God, and all these other things will be added unto you."[8]

I think this is not only true for our hopes and dreams, but ultimately for our calling and spiritual gifting. We must be willing to allow God to gift us as He sees fit, for whatever purpose He sees fit, at any time He sees fit.

Folks, being a pastor was never on my radar. I mean, seriously, who would want to behave that well over the course of their lifetime? But here I am, after 25 years of ministry. I still get to play music – a whole lot. Better yet, I get to play it with my family. We often play together in Charity's various worship services. When you trust God, your gifting empowers your calling, and your calling becomes your blessing.

In addition, even as my natural passions and gifts were animated for God's service, a deeper spiritual gift emerged. The gift of preaching and teaching. Sharing the Word of God with people on a weekly basis is an awesome responsibility and privilege. I

---

7 | 1 Corinthians 14
8 | Matthew 6:33

didn't know I had this gift. It manifested itself when, early in my ministry path, the Sr. Pastor I served alongside asked me to preach in his stead one week at worship. It probably wasn't the prettiest sermon in the world, but there was enough there that the gift was recognized. Then it was nurtured. Eventually it was affirmed, empowered and released. At the age of 49, I am guessing I have probably preached around 1,600 messages – over 2,400, if you include teaching sessions.

On the night when that imperfect group prayed imperfectly for the Holy Spirit to fill an imperfect young man – God showed up. Not with tongues, but with the gift of preaching. The Spirit planted in me like a seed, allowing it to germinate, take root, and finally emerge when the conditions were right.

Oh … the mystery. *Sehnsucht.*

The Supernatural Gifts:
God Follows Through On A Deal

In March of 1990, I made a deal with God about the supernatural gifts. "You have to knock me out with it so I know it's you God," I said. I didn't realize God would take me quite so literally.

It was June of 2001 and I had been working at Charity for 10 years. I was in the process of completing my Master's of Divinity from Fuller Theological Seminary and was on campus in Pasadena taking a leadership course from Dr. Bobby Clinton. In the middle of class one day, I suddenly received what felt like a vision. Immediately I began drawing a picture. It was a tree, and the tree was Charity. I received all kinds of interesting details about future ministries and ministers, including my own future at Charity.[9] These details filled three out of the four major branches of the tree. I have to say, some of what I wrote down was pretty interesting.

Once the frenetic writing had died down, I immediately challenged my own experience. Was this really a vision from God,

---

9 | At that time, Charity was still a reluctant member of the ELCA. Because Fuller was not a specifically Lutheran seminary, the ELCA would not recognize my education, effectively eliminating me from consideration as a Lutheran pastor, much less a pastor at Charity.

or was it just a burst of wishful thinking based upon my own natural creativity? I wasn't sure. But, I had an idea ...

Prior to traveling to Pasadena, I had seen on the TV show "The 700 Club" a story of a charismatic South Korean pastor named Che Ahn doing amazing ministry in Pasaden. Given my past experiences with charismatic stuff, I would have normally just moved on except for one bit of information that came forth. Che Ahn was Doctor Che Ahn. He had received his PhD from Fuller Theological Seminary. This immediately instilled in me a sense of trust and credibility, and I endeavored to meet him. I emailed him one week before coming to Fuller. Now I had an interesting reason to talk to him.

I attended his church that weekend with the agenda of pulling him aside and having him pray with me about my 'vision.' Sounded like a good plan, huh? Well ... you know our best-laid plans often go. Anyway ...

I arrived to find his church met in a very large, old school auditorium. I would say there were probably about 2,000 people in attendance. Now, I had been exposed to a fair amount of charismatic worship up until that point, but his church took things to a different level. Suffice it to say, I was thinking the whole idea was a mistake, and that I should go, when Dr. Ahn got up to preach.

It was stunning. Not because he was a dynamic speaker, but because the Holy Spirit just spoke so clearly and plainly through him. His theology was rock solid, his preaching simple and biblical. After he finished, he invited people to come to the front for prayer. It was an avalanche of humanity. I was humbled by the sheer humility and faith this South Korean sub-culture demonstrated.

I got in line, angling my way towards Dr. Ahn. When I stepped up to him, I quickly explained to him who I was (the student who emailed him), and that I needed prayer for this vision I had received. I hadn't even finished before he raised his right hand up toward my forehead and began praying – not in tongues or anything – just praying. He didn't even touch me.

Five seconds into his prayer, I was laying on the floor.

I didn't know what hit me. The sensation was like warm electricity, temporarily crippling me, but without any pain whatsoever. I didn't pass out or lose consciousness in any way. For me, the experience was very brief and relatively inconspicuous. And yet ...

Immediately I sat up on my rear, hugging my legs. "What in the world just happened?" I stammered to myself. I had been slain in the Spirit – but did not speak in tongues, shake or do any of the other things worshippers around me were doing. I just sat there.

And then I realized ... the vision; the Spirit was confirming the vision. Not only that, God was making good on a deal I had made with him over a decade earlier. It was as if He was saying, "It's OK. I got this. Stay faithful, and I will take care of everything else – including where I want you."

I didn't go looking for a supernatural experience or the supernatural gifts, but they found me. They found me in God's way, in God's time, and for God's purposes. So, when people ask me what I think about the supernatural gifts, I affirm them, point to scripture as a guide for their use, and remind them "It's OK, Gods got this. Seek to serve Him in love and humility, and He will take care of the rest."

Resting in Mystery

It's now been over 15 years since that Sunday morning. Everything confirmed by the Spirit in that vision has since came true, including my own ordination as a pastor at Charity.

So ... do I believe the supernatural gifts of the Spirit are alive and well today? You bet I do. I believe it because it's biblical. I believe it because, despite misuse and messiness, I have experienced them firsthand. I believe it because everyday I run up against my own inadequacies and limitations, which confirm that no amount of ministry can be achieved in our own power. I believe it, because I still see lives changed.

And, like C.S. Lewis, I believe it as I believe the sun has risen. Not only because I see it, but because by it, I see everything else.

I believe it because we were wired for mystery, and God is more than happy to oblige.

Sehnsucht.

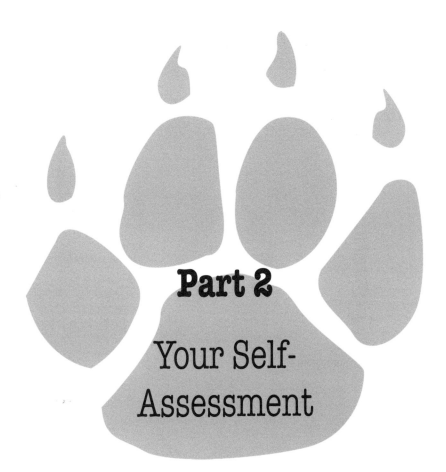

Part 2

Your Self-Assessment

Assessment Part 1: Your Raw Material

"Natural abilities are like natural plants; they need pruning by study."

Francis Bacon

Welcome To The Assessment.
Glad You Made It!

For the next four chapters you will be engaging in the participation portion of this book. I know … I know … I said I don't like assessments. Well, that's not fully true. I don't like incomplete assessments. I don't like assessments that make presumptions, forcing people into already constructed boxes. I don't like assessments that don't account for the dynamic aspect of the future.

A great example would be when my younger son Jordan took a vocational assessment at his school during his 8th grade year. Now Jordan has some interesting raw material; he is naturally a people person, good at conversation and reading people's emotions. He also loves video games, sports, music, and hunting. He has shown an interest in baking, and desires to learn his dad's master grilling skills. Though he is not great at using tools, he does like to mow. He has also shown an interest in being his own boss.

What was the assessment's final vocational conclusion?
Hang Gliding Instructor.

Are you kidding me? Now do you see why I am a bit skeptical of assessments?

This is why I am being careful with the assessment you are about to take. The goal is not to categorize you, but rather to lead and prompt you to honestly look at yourself; your raw material, your resources, your passions, and your pain. We will look for potential intersection points of those four areas, and then ask how those points might serve a need somewhere. That last area, pain, is one of the things that make this gifting assessment different. Most assessments either overemphasize pre-existing categories, or they overemphasize your passions. But the truth is that pain is one of the most significant motivators in our lives. You will be asked to examine the events in your life that have left scars, the things you see in the world that break your heart, and the things that you are not comfortable doing. We are at our most Christ-like, not when we run from pain, but when we acknowledge it and run toward it, bringing to bear our gifting for the sake of those who need hope, encouragement and healing.

You will be getting used to the following assessment graphic. This is a visual way of seeing our whole selves, and how our God-given shape and calling can be targeted.

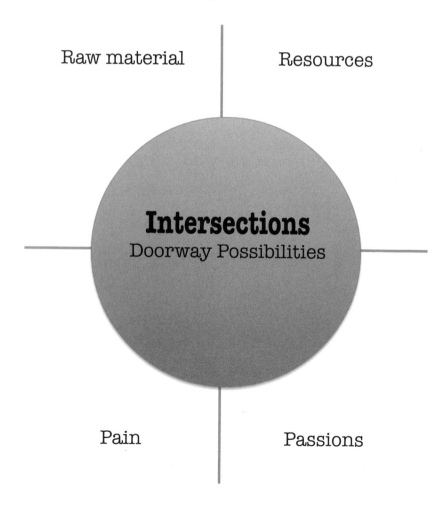

Part 1: Assessing Your Raw Material

In my sophomore year of college, I was a local basketball celebrity.[1]

Though quiet throughout most of my high school years, my career really bloomed at the collegiate level. I was a starting forward on a junior college team that made a habit out of beating up four-year schools. I wasn't the best player or the most talented, but I had carved my niche through hard-nosed, smart, tough play. Our team was nationally ranked, and I was being recognized as an All-State and All-Conference player. My picture was in the newspaper sport's section often, and I was recognized around town. I was, for the most part, a "local boy makes good" type of story.

Did I mention I had a younger brother?

Actually I have two younger brothers (Bob and Mike), but in this story I need to talk about the middle one, Bob. Anyway, back to the story ...

Bob was also good at basketball. Everything I had accomplished, he had accomplished even better. He was two years younger, so when I was a college standout, he was an All-State high school standout. The name 'Upgren' was mentioned either in the paper, or in TV sports stories nearly daily for a while. When Bob and I would show up at the YMCA together, nobody wanted to play against us.

One day, while waiting for a game together at the Y, Bob and I decided to play against each other, one-on-one. Now Bob was a better shooter, so I was used to him beating me in the occasional game of H-O-R-S-E, but in head-to-head games, I still tended to get the better of him, if for no other reason that I was just physically a little bigger and stronger. At this point, this dynamic was still true, but the gap had closed considerably.

The game began – one point per basket, two for three-pointers, first to 11 wins. The first contest, as expected was close. I would go up a couple; then Bob would hit a two-point shot. He would go up a point, then I would take him inside and overpower him – but

---

1 | Bismarck State College, Bismarck, ND.

not so easily as in the past. Buy the time the dust cleared, Bob had won the first game, 12-10 (you had to win by two).

"Lucky … ," I said, "Let's play again."

Game two went similar to the first; back and forth, but resulting in a second victory for Bob. The first game was no aberration. This bothered me … a lot. What made matters worse, a crowd had now gathered to watch. I was losing to my little brother – in public.

I insisted on one more game to save face, telling myself that if I played to my strengths, I could capture a win and my status as the top Upgren.

I'd like to tell you I won.
I'd like to tell you it was close.

Three in a row … I had lost three games in a row to my younger brother … for all to see. An undeniable seismic shift had occurred in the universe of the Upgren family. Bob had grown up – and all things being basically equal, showed that he was the better basketball player.

We both worked hard, but he had more talent.
We both had ability, but he had the better raw material.

We all have to understand and
come to peace with our raw material.

What Are You Naturally Good At?

As each one has received a special gift, employ it in serving one another as good stewards of the manifold grace of God.
1 Peter 4:10.

These are things that you are good at without any pro-longed training or practice. Some people could ride a bike the first time their dad let go, others like me, needed to crash two or three … or eight times.

Allow me to impose a further restriction; these are not necessarily things you like to do. For example, I was actually pretty good at math, but I don't actually like to do math. I'd rather watch paint dry than do Algebra.

So ... let's review.

You are naturally good at these things.
You didn't have to get training or practice a bunch to be good at them.
You don't necessarily like these things.

OK, let's explore ... put a checkmark next to anything that describes you.

Intellectual ... are you good at:

- Reading and understanding various kinds of books
- Doing research or writing clear and understandable reports
- Analyzing material and seeing good things and flaws
- Science and/or math, engineering, architecture. Does it come pretty easy to you?
- History – do you seem to understand the significance or people and events? Are you able to see the relevance of past events for today?
- Teaching – are you good at helping people understand things?
- Healing – are you good at helping people to feel better when they are either hurting physically, emotionally or spiritually?
- Miscellaneous: anything else in this area the list may have missed: _____

_____

Business ... are you good at:

- Managing people in a way the makes them effective and feel valued?

- Making and managing money – do you have a knack for seeing where money can be made or grown?
- Coming up with ideas, services or products that can help people
- Technology – creating or managing hardware or software that can enhance people's lives or the effectiveness of organizations
- Accounting – managing money for accuracy and integrity
- Miscellaneous: anything else in this area the list may have missed: _____

_____

Leadership ... are you good at:

- Motivating people and helping to optimize their potential
- Team building – getting the right people in the right places for the right reasons, all working toward the right goals
- People skills – do you have an innate ability to sense how people are feeling (EQ), and articulate those feelings to build consensus
- Vision – do you have the ability to see how things could be different or better in the future, and articulate that effectively
- Public service – do you seem to be good at working in environments that involve goals, objectives, and environments common to government
- Miscellaneous: anything else in this area the list may have missed: _____

_____

Physical ... are you good at:

- Are you good at outdoor sports or activities such as hunting, fishing, boating, running, etc
- Work related to farming or ranching – do you have knack for fixing machinery, physical structures, agriculture, or fencing. Are you good at working with animals?

- Working with your hands – using various kinds of tools. Do you have an ability to understand and repair things?
- Maintaining, cleaning, and managing facilities
- Understanding the nature and the environment, and seeing ways to steward and manage these things effectively
- Miscellaneous: anything else in this area the list may have missed: _____

Creative ... are you good at:

- Music – writing, singing, performing on instruments, recording, using music in drama, healing, or worship
- Drama – writing, acting, stage management, technology, promotion, production
- Literature – writing short stories or novels, teaching, adapting to TV, Film or stage, teaching or encouraging through fiction or non-fiction
- Painting or sculpting, teaching, etc.
- Speaking – motivational speaking, preaching, teaching seminars
- Miscellaneous: anything else in this area the list may have missed: _____

Next Step: Gather the Check Marks

For your next step please re-draw on paper (it doesn't have to be perfect) the large assessment graph at the beginning of this chapter. You can use it as a bookmark going forward. In the area labeled "Raw Material," write down your top five checkmarks or miscellaneous notes. I know that sifting these down can be difficult, but we need to avoid getting too broad.

If there is a tie for #5 between two things – chose the one you enjoy more. If you don't have five items – don't fret. If you don't have at least two, go back over this section with someone you know and trust – my guess is you might be underselling yourself.☺

After you have finished filling out that section of the assessment graphic, return back to this spot to finish the chapter.

The Hope Expressed Through Raw Material

Philosopher Al Wolters writes,

> "The earth had been completely unformed and empty; in the six-day process of development, God had formed it and filled it – but not completely. People must now carry on the work of development: by being fruitful they fill it even more; by subduing it they must form it even more … as God's representatives (we) carry on where God left off. But this now is to be a human development of the earth. The human race will fill the earth with its own kind, and it will form the earth for its own kind. From now on the development of the created earth will be societal and cultural in nature." [2]

We must resist the fallacy that some areas of human endeavor are innately more spiritual than others. We must remember that from the very beginning (Genesis 1 and 2) humanity was given work as part of its very God-given identity. Thus all work, when in harmony with Gods' creation and values, is innately spiritual.

The businessman's calling is just as spiritual as the pastor's. The custodian's calling is just as spiritual as the teacher's. The veterinarian's calling is just as spiritual as the musician's.

In his book, *Every Great Endeavor*, Tim Keller points out that God invited mankind into the creative process through the calling of culture-making. This mandate is expressed in Genesis 1:28:

> God blessed them and said to them, "Be fruitful and increase in number; fill the earth and subdue it. Rule over the fish in the sea and the birds in the sky and over every living creature that moves on the ground."

---

2 | *Creation Regained; A Transforming View of the World.*

God placed Adam and Eve into a garden – but not as passive tenants. God wanted them to actively steward, or manage, this garden in a way that was consistent with His character and values. Keller writes,

> "If we are to be God's image-bearers with regard to creation, then we will carry on his pattern of work. His world is not hostile, so that it needs to be beaten down like an enemy. Rather, its potential is undeveloped, so it needs to be cultivated like a garden. So we are not to relate to the world as park rangers, whose job is not to change their space, but to preserve things as they are. Nor are we to "pave over the garden" of the created world to make a parking lot. No, we are to be **gardeners** who take an active stance toward their charge. They do not leave the land as it is. They rearrange it in order to make it most fruitful, to draw the potentialities for growth and development out of the soil …"

Keller goes on to share a cogent example of how calling must be understood rightly. In today's American culture, there is a strange tension between prosperity and revulsion for the business that makes prosperity possible. This can wreak havoc on the sense of calling for people engaged in business and commerce.

> "Fuller Seminary president Richard Mouw once addressed a number of bankers in New York City. He pointed them to Genesis and showed that God was a creator/investor who made the world as a home for kinds of creativity. Mouw urged his audience to think of God as an investment banker. He leveraged his resources to create a whole world of new life. In the same way, what if you see a human need not being met, you see a talent or resource that can meet that need, and you then invest your resources – at your risk and cost – so that the need is met and result is new jobs, new products, and better quality of life? What you are doing, Mouw concluded, is actually God-like.

> "After the address, many in the audience said, 'Could you talk to my minister about this? He thinks that all I care about is making money.' "

Pastors who think of business in such broad-brushed negative ways are guilty of the mistake we talked about in an earlier chapter – they "churchify" calling in ways that are not ultimately biblical.

All work done in the name of God honors our raw material, employing it in acts of praise that are staggering in their beauty and diversity. Remember, God himself didn't come as a religious leader, He came as a carpenter.

When we use our raw material in this way, we become agents of hope in the world. God-given raw material is stubborn, if used consistently, it never really goes away. It may fade somewhat in its glory, but it always persists as a testimony to the goodness of the one who gives such gifts.

John Ortberg points out several examples of this,

> "When he was an old man, the master painter Henri Matisse was crippled by arthritis. Wrapping his fingers around a brush was painful; painting was agony. Someone asked him why he kept painting. He answered, 'The pain goes away; the beauty endures.' That is hope.

> "Pablo Casals continued to practice the cello five hours a day even though he was recognized as the world's greatest cellist, even when he had grown ancient enough that the effort exhausted him. Someone asked him what made him do it. 'I think I'm getting better.' That is hope.

> "Lewis Smedes writes that when Michelangelo was laboring day after day painting the ceiling of the Sistine Chapel, he grew so discouraged that he resolved to quit.

> "As the dusk darkened the always-shadowed Sistine Chapel, Michelangelo, weary, sore, and doubtful, climbed down the ladder from his scaffolding where he'd been lying on his back since dawn painting the chapel ceiling. After eating a lonely dinner, he wrote a sonnet to his aching body. The last line [was] . . . I'm no painter.

> "But when the sun shone again, Michelangelo got up from his bed, climbed up his scaffold, and labored another day on his magnificent vision of the Creator.

What pushed him up the ladder? Hope."[3]

Don't think your raw material doesn't matter. It does. Remember, God does amazing things with raw material.

How about we start with yours?

---

3 | *If You Want To Walk On Water You Have To Get Out Of The Boat.*

Assessment Part 2: Your Resources

*"Start where you are.
Use what you have. Do what you can."*

Arthur Ashe

Have you ever played poker?

Now – I'm not suggesting anyone give up their day job and try to make a living exploring their spiritual gifts in the gambling world (there is a reason the House always wins folks).

I'm talking about just playing cards for fun. On warm summer nights, I love to get a fire going on our deck overlooking the Missouri River, and sit and play cards with my boys. No TV, no gadgets … just being together under the stars playing cards. Sometimes it's poker.

Now … my brother Bob is a different story. When he was in his teens, Bob didn't need a summer job because he had his poker buddies, Doug, Tim and Mike. Bob was really good at poker. Doug, Tim, and Mike were not so good at poker. Bob would bring home more in poker winnings every week than I made slaving in the back kitchen at the local Arby's.

Do you know what a poker face is?

There is skill involved with winning in poker, and one of the skills has to do with learning how to read your opponent's body language. They call it a "tell," if a person is blutting, their body language, often a facial expression, will tell you. Bob was super good at this. It drove Doug, Tim and Mike crazy. Bob knew when they were bluffing, and knew when they had a good hand … he could "tell," A good poker face hides your "tolls."

One night while playing, Tim finally had enough. After losing yet another pot to Bob, he announced that he was going to the bathroom. When returned, he was wearing a Halloween mask – one those old-school plastic masks with the rubber band. Tim was Richie Rich. Not to be outdone, Doug and Mike immediately requested equal treatment. Tim obliged. The next thing you know Bob was sitting at the poker table dealing cards to Richie Rich, Jaws the Shark, and the Fonz from "Happy Days." Suffice it to say that even though Bob got a huge laugh out the scenario, it did even the odds.

Martin Luther believed that God wore masks for the same reason – to even the odds – not for himself, but for his people. Luther believed that God was constantly at work providing and resourcing his people under the cover of "masks."

> *"What else is all our work to God – whether in the fields, in the garden, in the city, in the house, in war, or in government – but just such a child's performance, by which He wants to give His gifts in the fields, at home, and everywhere else? These are the masks of God, behind which He wants to remain concealed and do all things."*[1]

There are masks, but this is no poker game. Luther desires to drive home the mysterious truth that if we actually believe what scripture says, we must act in concert with the idea that we work for a master who has limitless resources.

Too often, when seeking to move in our God-given calling and giftedness, we assume resourcing limits that don't exist. We become conditioned over time by worldly ways of thinking and forget that the LORD "owns the cattle on a thousand hills."[2]

Psychologist and author Mark Noll reminds us of this all-encompassing resourcefulness of God,

> *"Who, after all, made the world of nature, and then made possible the development of sciences through which we find out more about nature? Who formed the universe of human interactions, and so provided the raw material for politics, economics, sociology, and history? Who is the source of harmony, form, and narrative pattern, and so lies behind all artistic and literary possibilities? ... Who maintains moment by moment the connections between what is in our minds and*

---

1 | Pelikan, *Luther's Works*, Volume 14, p.96.
2 | Psalm 50:10

*what is in the world ... The answer in every case is the same –
God did it. And God does it."[3]*

Noll says it well, but this is not new thinking. His thoughts are merely
echoes of the words of Paul in his letter to the church in Colossae,

*"For in Him all things were created, things in heaven and on
earth, visible and invisible, whether thrones or dominions or rulers
or authorities. All things were created through Him and for Him.
He is before all things, and in Him all things hold together."[4]*

We make our God too small. He is able to resource His purposes
in ways that go beyond our limited reach. We often either forget
that, or we don't really believe it to begin with. The key, however,
is not to simply believe that anything can be yours for the taking,
but to seek to align ourselves with God's purposes. The more we
submit to His Kingdom, the more His resources become available
in the day-to-day exercise of our calling and giftedness.

This is why reading Scripture is so important. How can you know
the heart of God if you don't read His love letter? How can you
know the mind of God if you don't read His story? Writing to the
new believers in Rome, whose previous allegiance and service
had been to Caesar, the Apostle Paul says,

*"Do not conform to the pattern of this world, but be transformed
by the renewing of your mind. Then you will be able to test and
approve what God's will is – his good, pleasing and perfect
will."[5]*

Starting With What You Already Possess

In his wonderful message *Drops Like Stars*,[6] author Rob Bell
shares a personal observation regarding the biblical difference
between owning and possessing. Rob is an amateur musician,
and loves to collect vintage guitars. One day, a friend of Rob's,
Joey, visited and noticed his prized Rickenbacker 330 sitting in the

3 | *The Scandal of the Evangelical Mind*, p.51.
4 | Colossians 1:16-17
5 | Romans 12:2
6 | I do not agree with all of Rob's theology; however, I do find his writings and
talks thought-provoking and helpful in many ways.

corner. Tenderly picking it up, Joey began to play the instrument, coaxing music out of it in ways that Rob simply couldn't do. Rob would go on to say that though he was the legal owner of the guitar, Joey 'possessed' it in ways Rob could not experience.

Paul would refer to this paradox,

> " ...(We are) poor, yet making many rich; having nothing, and yet possessing everything."[7]

As already illustrated, one aspect of "possessing" something is our ability to actually use it fully in the way it was intended – to apply to it what the Greeks called "Logos"[8] – an object's design or reason for existing. This is why Joey, as a superior musician, possessed the guitar in ways that Rob couldn't.

A second way of possessing something in the sense Paul alludes to is when we take what we already have and redirect it's use more fully towards God's purposes. When Pam and I purchased Providence Ranch, we could have merely been owners, using the property and horses for our own personal enjoyment. This would not necessarily be bad, but it would fall short of biblically possessing the ranch. Instead, after about a two-year period of getting used to ranch life, Pam and I began to share the blessings of the ranch with other kids and families in the community – particularly those with special needs. As we have slowly continued to do this, God has faithfully opened up a broader array of resources for our use.

We are not called simply to receive God's blessings - We are called to share them.

As you move forward now with assessing your resources, I cannot encourage you enough to think about this idea of possessing in the biblical sense, and how you might be able to redirect resources you already have towards God's purposes.

---

7 | 2 Corinthians 6:10
8 | This is the word John would use for Jesus in John 1. As the Logos, Jesus was the ultimate reason for existence – the source of all things.

Resource Inventory

Three basic areas are worthy of evaluation; Financial and Hard Assets, Education and Training, and People. Once again, put a check by areas that reflect your situation, and then write down the top five in the designated section of the graph at the back of the book.

Financial and Hard Assets:

- Discretionary, liquid money in the form of savings or investments.
- Discretionary money in the form of liquid life insurance policies.
- Property that could be donated or liquidated.
- Annuity cash from settlements or prize winnings.
- Property that could be used for ministry "as is."
- Vacation property that could be used "as is" or liquidated.
- Vehicles or recreational vehicles or boats that could be used "as is" (i.e. you love to fish, so you decide to start a ministry taking kids fishing, or allow your boat to be used in a ministry like this), donated, or liquidated.
- Inheritance assets that could be used, donated or liquidated.
- Miscellaneous: _____

_____

Education and Training:

(This is training that can be either re-applied toward Kingdom purposes, or enhanced toward Kingdom purposes – i.e., a bachelor's degree can be parlayed into seminary-level ministry training – or can be donated to already existing ministries.)

- Post graduate degree.
- College degree.
- Vocational or technical training.

- Special or adjunct training (i.e., I have special training as a pre-marital counselor I can use to help couples.)
- Special licensing (i.e., CPA, Law, OTR or Bus-driving licenses, etc.).
- Miscellaneous: _____

_____

People:

This would entail people in your life who might be able to help you in your pursuit of your calling, dream, and gifting (i.e., remember from a previous chapter – the waitress who wanted to be a nurse who realized her mother could babysit her kids so she could go back to school.)

- Retired parents or siblings who have time to help you.
- Family or friends who have special skills to help you.
- Family or friends who have relevant education or training to help you.
- Family, friends, or acquaintances who have assets that could help you.
- Fellow Christians in the community who have special assets, position, businesses, or skills that could help you.
- Churches in the community who could provide guidance, assets, financial resources, or volunteers that could help you.
- Media people who could make your ministry, dream, or calling known.
- Miscellaneous: _____

_____

Asking For Help in Both Directions

It can be hard to ask for help. I know.

But trust me, rugged American individualism[9] is not the path of the called and gifted in God's economy. We must be humble enough to ask for help – in both directions. In prayer we appeal to God, not just for resources, but also for transformation along the way. However, we also embrace the truth that God wears masks, and will work in the people around you as well. To ask them for help with a pure and humble heart is to ask God Himself.

Proverbs 16:1-3 says,

> "To humans belong the plans of the heart,
>   but from the Lord comes the proper answer of the tongue.
>
> "All a person's ways seem pure to them,
>   but motives are weighed by the Lord.
>
> "Commit to the Lord whatever you do,
>   and he will establish your plans."

We must forsake a "bucket" mentality, and latch on to a "funnel" mentality. In doing so, we become vessels through which God's blessings flow through, working His will in us, and through us to the surrounding world. Paul would articulate this in Romans 12:1,

> "Therefore, I urge you, brothers and sisters, **in view of God's mercy,** to offer your bodies as a living sacrifice, holy and pleasing to God—this is your true and proper worship."

This is how we allow God to become bigger. In pleasing Him above all others by serving others, He begins to open up the vast array of His resources – often in ways that are surprising and unpredictable.

This is the way of those who are called. This is the paradox of those who are gifted.

---

9 | Don't get me wrong – I'm very proud to be an American. But the myth of the self-made success is neither American at its heart, nor biblical.

In C.S. Lewis' book *Prince Caspian*, one of the children, Lucy, comes upon Aslan, the Christ-figure of the Narnia stories, after a pro-longed absence.

"Aslan, you're bigger," says Lucy.

"That is because you are older, little one," answered He.

"Not because you are?"

"I am not. But every year you grow, you will find me bigger."

It's not poker.

There is no gamble – only the appearance of it.

You don't need to own anything, but it is your destiny to possess all things.

Just trust the one behind the mask.

Assessment Part 3: Your Passion

"The most powerful weapon on earth is the human soul on fire."

Ferdinand Foch

Have you ever been in a conversation with someone that just wasn't happening? You can just tell the 'connection' isn't there.

As someone who communicates for a living, it is imperative to have the ability to read your audience – to be sensitive to whether or not this connection is happening. This is true whether your audience is 1 or 1,000. When the connection isn't happening, the signs silently scream at you:

- Wandering and intermittent eye contact – rubbing of the eyes
- Yawning and persistent shifting of the derrière (that's 'butt' in French) in the chair
- Distracted tinkering with programs, bulletins or smart phones
- Body posture that is reclining or leaning away from the speaker
- For the listener it will seem as if Einstein's time continuum will come into play: a 15-minute message will feel like 3 hours. The listener will actually appear visibly older afterwards.
- IN EXTREME CASES: A trance-like fascination with the contents of the nose

Likewise, when you are tapping into something that your audience is passionate about, the connection will spark and flash with life – the body language will be animated and engaged. Rather than monologue, the interaction will truly be dialogue.

I remember a great example of this.

His name was William. He was a 17-year-old boy in our church. I was the youth director in those days, and I was making an attempt to "connect."

William wasn't particularly active in our youth group, and so my agenda of this meeting was simply to get to know William, and let him know that we cared about him despite his inactivity at church.

Boy ... the first half hour of that conversation was tough. His body language was clearly saying, "I want be somewhere else." I'm pretty sure he was entertaining in his head employing the "splash and dash" strategy to achieve a get-away (excusing himself to use the bathroom, and then never coming back). Cold conversations are hard, and I can't say that I blamed him.

However, this wasn't my first difficult conversation with a teenager, and I had attained some useful tools in turning the tide of such meetings. I started asking him questions – all kinds of them. These were questions designed to help me find out what made William tick. I covered the normal teenage male territory; sports, girls, hunting, fishing, girls, cars, girls, summer plans, girls ... you get the picture. I was hitting a dead end at every turn, so I got desperate – I just asked him, "William what do you love to do? What makes you feel alive when you are doing it?"

I'll never forget his answer, "Cooking."

Before you could say Wolfgang Puck I was immersed into a conversational world of cookery, recipes and sauce theory. As if I'd pushed a button, William suddenly was awake and attentive; eyes wide open and fixed on mine, hands illustratively flailing about in response to each question I posed. In short, William came alive.

Passion As Deep Gladness

What makes you come alive?

- What gets your heart beating faster (in a good way)?
- What kind of activity actually seems to give you energy?

- What makes time seem to fly by when you are doing it?

- What puts you in the 'zone' – that place where your concentration is heightened, your focus sharp, and you feel connected to reality and in the moment?

- What activity occupies your thoughts, even when you aren't doing it?

Author Max Lucado calls this place a person's divine "sweet spot."[1]

One of my spiritual gifts is being able to spot that 'thing' in other people. I can't tell you how it turns my crank to see other people come alive. When I see it in other people, I actually get a visceral, emotional reaction – as if time is standing still – and I stand in awe of the mystery of how God shapes each person in special ways.

Divine sweet spots are contagious – they can't help but benefit the people around them – in fact, they were designed that way! Divine sweet spots are not just for the rich, the famous, or privileged. They are hidden in the inner heart of each person, awaiting the opportunity to be released fully. That is the beauty of sweet spots – they are literally all around us, as numerous and diverse as people themselves.

I've seen the sweet spot in action. I've seen it in my wife as she works with kids and horses on our ranch. I've seen it in my good friend Bob, a band director, as he guides kids into the joys and mystery of playing music together. I've seen it in Jim, a local mechanic, as he takes his knowledge about cars and uses it to spend time and build confidence in struggling teenagers.

This is exciting stuff. It is most exciting when you see it emerge in someone for the very first time, like catching that magic moment when a flower just starts to bloom.

I most recently was privileged to witness this kind of emergence in my own son, Josh. Like a lot of teenagers these days, Josh has entered the college years still a bit undefined about what his calling and vocation might be. He is only 19 so that is OK, but once you start paying tuition, the stakes raise considerably. After

---

1 | Found in his 2005 book entitles *Cure for the Common Life: Living in Your Sweet Spot.*

a disappointing experience with electrical lineman school, I asked my son what he would do if money were not an issue.

"Park Ranger," he said, without even hesitating.

"Why don't you pursue that then?" I asked.

"Because you can't support a family on what it pays," He answered.

Granted, you're not likely going to grace the cover of *Forbes* working in America's great outdoors. However, given the season of life Josh finds himself in, he could afford to start with passion and work toward the practical concerns. So we started with his passion.

Josh loves the outdoors. Josh loves drama and music. Josh loves history. Josh loves his home state of North Dakota. With all these factors in consideration, and with a little help from some friends, we were able to find him a summer job that allowed him to dip his toe in this vocational pool; *Park Interpreter at Fort Lincoln State Park in Mandan, ND*

With this job, Josh would:

- Work outdoors within the park system
- Use his love of history and drama, giving 'in character' tours to park visitors
- Tap into his love of his home state
- Get his foot in the door towards a potential career track
- Efficiently explore whether this might be the right direction

Did I mention how excited I get when I see someone tap into their passion? Well, imagine how I felt when I beheld this moment with my own son. That summer Pam and I visited Fort Lincoln to see how Josh was doing. As he led our group on a tour of General George Custer's home, dressed in Union Soldier period attire, I marveled at how my "little boy" brought it all to life, dramatically weaving together history and humor. I thought my chest was going to burst with pride.

I know, I know ... I am biased. But remember, recognizing the divine sweet spot is one of my gifts. I know it when I see it ... *and I saw it.*

This is one of the reasons why we say God is good. He doesn't ask you to sacrifice your core being to serve Him, he asks you to *dedicate* your core being to serve Him. When we align ourselves with Him in this way, we come alive. God is not only glorified by the work of pastors, but of an endless array of vocations such as doctors, public servants, sales people, entrepreneurs, homemakers, and yes ... park rangers.

Consider the diversity of people God used for his glory in scripture: Kings (Cyrus), queens (Esther), prophets (Isaiah), musicians (Psalms), farmers (Amos), fishermen (Peter), tax collectors (Matthew), doctors (Luke), shepherds (David), soldiers (Roman Centurion), tentmakers (Paul), midwives (see Exodus), etc. The vocations of all of these examples were either employed directly into God's purposes (i.e., King Cyrus used his authority to free the Jewish people to return to their land), or indirectly shaped the impact of these people (i.e., the Roman Centurion understood the relationship between faith and authority in a way that impressed Jesus).

Exploring and targeting one's passion is an exciting and challenging endeavor. However, there is another side to the concept of passion that also needs to be considered ...

Passion as Suffering

The word *passion* is a double-edged sword. It is not only understood as something which makes us come alive, but also as something for which we are willing to suffer. In fact, the Latin word for passion, *pati*, literally means "to suffer." This is what separates true passion from a mere hobby.

This is why the agonizing work of Jesus Christ on the cross is called "*The Passion.*" The core being and purpose of Christ was to rescue humanity from its own self-destructive rebellion – and this rescue would require the ultimate suffering to accomplish.

Alongside the animating indicators of passion come the suffering indicators. When considering soberly whether something is truly your passion and purpose you must not only ask whether is makes you come alive, but also:

- Am I willing to invest time and resources into this?
- Am I willing to sacrifice comfort for this?
- Am I willing to sacrifice fun things, in exchange for good things?
- Am I willing to work at and pursue this even when I don't feel like it?
- Am I willing to risk failure so that my passion might grow and mature into something that benefits others?
- Am I willing to endure criticism and discouragement for this?

If something is your passion, you will willingly embrace suffering for its own sake.

The fact that I am writing this book, rather than sunning myself on my deck overlooking the river, is an indication of passion. But even more, the fact that I have the *freedom* to write this book, as an expression of religious faith, is evidence that I have benefited from someone else's passion. We live in a nation that is unique in its reverence and protection of religious freedom. This didn't happen by accident – it was the result of passion – specifically the passion of our founding fathers – Washington, Jefferson, Franklin, Hamilton, etc. They didn't just have an idea for a new nation; they were passionately captured by a vision for a new nation. This vision occupied their dreams, consumed their waking thoughts and moved them collectively to suffer greatly to see it come to reality.[2] This collective expression of passion is articulated beautifully at the close of the Declaration of Independence.

> "And for the support of this Declaration, with a firm reliance on the protection of divine Providence, we mutually pledge to each other our Lives, our Fortunes and our sacred Honor."

Is your passion something into which you are willing to pour your life, invest your fortune, and build your honor upon? Moreover, are you willing to do this thing for the sake of others, for the benefit of your neighbor and the glory of God? Embracing both sides of

---

2 | John Hancock, for example, committed immense amounts of his personal wealth to the cause of the war. See revolutionarywararchives.com.

passion is essential for identifying what it personally looks like in you.

Remember, if it's only about fun, then it's merely a hobby.
But if you are, willing to sacrifice for it, suffer for it, and serve others with it, then its passion.

Passion Inventory

So, at the risk of being redundant, let's revisit those defining questions and write down some answers. Take your time. Be thoughtful. Be prayerful. Be honest.

Passion: What Makes You Come Alive?

- What gets your heart beating faster (in a good way)?
- What kind of activity actually seems to give you energy?
- What makes time seem to fly by when you are doing it?
- What puts you in the "zone" – that place where your concentration is heightened, your focus sharp, and you feel connected to reality and in the moment?
- What activity occupies your thoughts, even when you aren't doing it?

Passion: Am I Willing to Suffer?

- Am I willing to invest time and resources into this?
- Am I willing to sacrifice comfort for this?
- Am I willing to sacrifice fun things, in exchange for good things?
- Am I willing to work at and pursue this even when I don't feel like it?
- Am I willing to risk failure so that my passion might grow and mature into something that benefits others?
- Am I willing to endure criticism and discouragement for this?

Passion: The Practical Questions

- Am I good enough at this activity to actually be of service to, or somehow otherwise bless others?

- Is this an activity that I can be legitimately educated, trained or mentored in?

- Is this something I can realistically expect to make a living at, or do on the side in addition to a responsible job?

- Have other people, who I know will be honest, seen and affirmed this passion in me? Have they encouraged me to pursue it further?[3]

Conclusion: Passion as Responsibility
(DO NOT SKIP THIS PART!)

Let's be honest. Not everyone in this world has the opportunity to entertain or explore the questions in this book. As American Christians, we are blessed beyond measure to live in a land in which the possibility and resources to dream and shape our lives is a reality. This is simply not true in other places.

In his book, I, World Vision CEO David Stearns describes what would happen to our lives if just one daily reality we take for granted, clean and available water, disappeared.

> "Most of you began this morning with a hot, clean shower. You brushed your teeth, filled a glass with water, and took a few vitamins. (The older I get, the more pills I seem to take.) Perhaps you brewed a cup of coffee or drank a glass of juice with breakfast. And each day, you run your washing machines and dishwashers, and take your toilets for granted.

> "You probably have one, two, or even three bathrooms in your home. You may also have a sprinkler system to water your lawn and garden. Your refrigerator is filled with cold drinks, bottled water, and maybe even ice-cold water dispensed from its door. If you have children, they probably haven't spent even

---

3 | A good test for this would be to eliminate any affirmation from family. Do you have friends, acquaintances, colleagues, or even better – professionals in your area of passion – that will affirm this in you.

one hour of their lives fetching water for the family to drink or to bathe with. And I'll wager that neither you nor your children have ever had a sick day due to unclean water—unless you have traveled to another country and picked up one of many waterborne bacteria or parasites.

"So now, as you did with hunger, I want you to imagine for a moment that when you wake up tomorrow, all of the water-related fixtures have been removed from your home. The sinks, toilets, bathtubs, and showers are gone. Dishwasher, washing machine, garden hoses, sprinklers—all gone. Let's say, though, that everything else about your home remains the same. Still, how would your life change with just this one difference?

Well, think about it. You would wake up wanting to use the toilet, take your hot shower, brush your teeth, swallow those vitamins, and fix breakfast—but you can't. What would you do? At first, you would be irritated by the minor inconvenience of having no showers, toilets, dishwasher, or washing machine—until it started to dawn on you that this is far more serious—a threat, actually, to your health, your family, even your survival. Finding a way to get water would begin to consume your life. Without food, you can live sometimes for weeks, but without water? Life as you know it would be transformed—and not in a good way."

Stearns goes on to describe the impact in terms of perspective: daily life would become about basic survival rather than privileged considerations of passion, calling and giftedness. All of your time and resources would be devoted to the bare essentials of staying alive.

"Tragically, living without water has even more dimensions. Thousands of hours are lost seeking and hauling water, especially by women. These are hours that could be spent earning an income or contributing to the well-being of the family and community. This same task affects children too: millions of them are unable to attend school because of the hours they spend fetching water. And because of the unsafe quality of their water, many who can go to school are chronically sick and struggle with learning. Some waterborne parasites—guinea worm, for example—can even result in crippling, and bacterial diseases such as trachoma can cause blindness.

"Despite the risks, women and children in developing countries invest two hundred million hours a day fetching water. That's equal to a full-time workforce of twenty-five million people fetching water eight hours a day, seven days a week! The men, as unremittingly ill as their wives and children, become less productive in their work, often reducing the agricultural output and food supply of the whole community. Those whose immune systems have been weakened by AIDS or tuberculosis are further ravaged by waterborne illnesses, and it is estimated that as many as one-half of the world's hospital beds are occupied by people with a water-related illness."

Why do I bring up this sobering picture? Is it some sort of guilt trip? No. But … it is a reminder that our blessings and gifts are to be pursued and exercised in such a way that more and more people can flourish. Calling and spiritual giftedness are to be employed in an infectious manner – bringing hope, healing, freedom, and opportunity to all of God's children across the world. Human suffering and oppression should not be a guilt-ridden deterrent to pursuing your calling, but rather a difference-making catalyst. The world needs people who are alive and ready to sacrifice and serve. The world needs people who are gifted in all varieties of vocations to bring blessing, security, healing, and a fighting chance to the masses.

The great leader Nelson Mandela, himself a former victim of injustice, said it best in his 1994 inaugural address.[4]

"Our deepest fear is not that we are inadequate. Our deepest fear is that we are powerful beyond measure. It is our light, not our darkness that most frightens us. We ask ourselves, Who am I to be brilliant, gorgeous, talented, fabulous? Actually, who are you not to be? You are a child of God. Your playing small does not serve the world. There is nothing enlightened about shrinking so that other people won't feel insecure around you. We are all meant to shine, as children do. We were born to make manifest the glory of God that is within us. It's not just in some of us; it's in everyone. And as we let our own light shine, we unconsciously give other people permission to do the same. As we are liberated from our own fear, our presence automatically liberates others."

4 | Mandela was quoting author Marianne Williamson from her book, *A Return To Love: Reflections on the Principles of A Course in Miracles.*

Passion is not the only factor in discerning your calling and spiritual gifts, but it is an important one. Connect to what makes you come alive – and be willing to suffer in the pursuit of its development, use and service. Live so that others might live. Sacrifice so that others might flourish. Serve so that others might find freedom and hope.

St. Theresa of Avila once said,

> "Christ has no body on earth but yours, no hands but yours,
> no feet but yours. Yours are the eyes through which
> Christ's compassion for the world is to look out;
> yours are the feet with which He is to go about doing good;
> and yours are the hands with which He is to bless us now."

Cooks, park rangers, founding fathers and everyday people like you ... this is the Kingdom of God. Your passion has a place. Apply today.

Assessment Part 4: Your Pain

"Although the world is full of suffering, it is also full of the overcoming of it."

Helen Keller

We have a strange relationship with pain these days.

We do everything we can to avoid pain. When I was about 8-years old I actually got my first filling ... *without Novacain* (that's right, I must have been a serious kick-butt kiddo). However, today, not only do we take for granted the wonders of Novacain, we also have gentle dentistry that uses sedation pills before the Novacain.

This is also now true with general anesthesia (another miracle in the avoidance of pain). A couple of years ago, I went into the hospital for an outpatient procedure. Not only were they going to administer general anesthesia, but they also used Lidacaine to minimize the pain experienced in getting the IV. It didn't work. The nurse injecting the IV must have been a beginner because after about four attempts and missing the vain on my hand, she had to yield to a veteran who got it right on the first try. Boy ... all of that painful effort to help me avoid pain. Uff da.

However, every man, if he has half a brain, will acknowledge that women have the market cornered on pain. We may spin tales of how much it hurt when we "turned that ankle in the basketball game," or "gashed my thigh with the chainsaw," or even "took one for the team right in the gonads during the softball game." But none of that – so we've been told ... over and over again – compares to giving birth to a child. Even with the miracle of the spinal tap, otherwise known as the epidural, the process of childbirth is dramatically more traumatic than anything the male gender can lay claim to. Mary Beth Sammons, in a blog entitled *"Funniest Things Overheard in the Delivery Room,"* shares some humorous examples of these pain-induced moments:

> *"There wasn't much that seemed funny during Maria L.'s five days of 'major contractions' leading up to her labor, but she*

laughs at her delirium and some of the statements she made. My mom told me that I asked the nurse repeatedly if 'it was hard to make people.' I also flipped out a few times about how I hated chicken and soccer.

"Another mom, Brittney, remembers being mortified when she was in the middle of her au naturel birth in the bathtub and 'I farted. I was so out of it, I just kept apologizing over and over again' to her mom and husband.

"In the 'things birth moms wish they hadn't said' category, Colby S. recalls, after 17 hours of labor, spilling out, 'Why can't we just lay eggs?' As she remembers, 'The doctor stopped in her tracks as well as the nurses and just looked at each other, and we all started laughing.'"

This pain avoidance endemic in our culture goes well beyond the physical variety. We avoid emotional pain too. Every kid in sports today gets a trophy and playgrounds have rubber matting on the ground. College campuses have 'safe zones' so students don't have to experience the 'micro-aggression' of an opinion different than their own. Men and women break up over a text rather than face each other and endure the awkward moment of rejection together.

I don't like pain either. So please understand my observations in this chapter are not some macho attempt to minimize the significance of pain. If fact, it is the opposite.

Catherine of Aragon said,

"None get to God but through trouble."[1]

I'm not suggesting that we should seek pain, or run after it in some sort of distorted attempt at martyrdom. However, I would suggest that our obsessive attempts to avoid all pain actually prevent us from benefiting from the right pain. It is a paradoxical truth:

In Christ, pain can sober us, mold us, and direct us.

---

1 | Catherine would know, having endured being the first wife of the infamously unfaithful and violent King Henry VIII.

The Pain of Birthing Blessings

It is my opinion that the most overlooked area of calling and spiritual gifting in people is their pain. Even more than passion, pain molds us and influences our behavior. When we try to 'do pain' without God, we fall into the pattern of avoidance, and end up denying ourselves the growth and perspective only He can bring about in us. In short, without God, pain often just influences our behavior, but with God, it can direct our calling.

Some of our greatest modern symbols of Christian love and compassion came in response to pain.

Clarissa began her life as one of the few women allowed to be a schoolteacher. By the time she reached the age of 40, war had descended upon her home and she witnessed countless horrors on the battlefield. Even as she felt compelled to come to the aid of the young soldiers who were wounded, sick and starving, she realized many of them were "her boys" – students from her own classrooms. Clarissa, though overwhelmed, immersed herself into the suffering, refusing to turn her eyes in the other direction.

Bill and Cathy were upset and frustrated with the local churches. Shortly after being ordained into the ministry, Bill sought to take seriously the messiness of reaching the poor, destitute and hungry with the gospel. However, he received little help from his ministerial colleagues who chose more traditional methods of evangelizing non-church going people. Their hearts broken over the lot of their "congregation," Bill and his wife Cathy left the organized church and struck out on their own.

April was hurting and confused. At an early age, she discovered that she suffered from Obsessive Compulsive Disorder. However, soon after several other diagnoses quickly followed, climaxing with Bipolar Disorder, she went through a period of trauma and homelessness, ultimately ending up isolated in a home specializing in caring for people with metal illness.

Danny felt like his life was aimless. Though talented, he struggled with the haunting sensation he wasn't fulfilling his purpose. His heart ached with unfulfilled longing. Desperate, one night he got on his knees and bartered a prayer to one of the patron saints of his Catholic faith. "Show me my way in life, and I will build you a shrine."

Danny, April, Clarissa, Bill and Cathy were moved to action in their lives not by musing over what their passion was alone (I call this divine belly button staring), but by experiencing brokenness in the world and genuinely wrestling with what their response should look like. Their pain became their guide to action. Their pain helped them to target their passion in ways that answered the internal cry of their hearts, "That isn't the way things ought to be!"

We all know this cry. At one moment or another, we have all uttered those words.

The Franciscan priest Richard Rohr notes that Native Americans have a tradition of leaving a blemish in one corner of a woven rug because that's where the Spirit enters.[2] Though God is not the ultimate source of suffering, He wastes nothing, entering into life's brokenness and blemishes in the person of Jesus Christ, and in the work of his people.

The Apostle Paul would echo this sentiment when he wrote to Jesus' followers in Corinth:

> *"Blessed be the God and Father of our Lord Jesus Christ, the Father of mercies and God of all comfort, who comforts us in all our affliction, so that we may be able to comfort those who are in any affliction, with the comfort with which we ourselves are comforted by God. For as we share abundantly in Christ's sufferings, so through Christ we share abundantly in comfort too."*[3]

Acknowledging our pain is the key to unlocking our calling and gifting. This can be pain we either experience directly, or vicariously (though others).

We are often tempted to think that our spiritual gifting and calling is about leading with what we are good at.

However, if you want to serve God, He will likely ask you to lead with your pain and brokenness.

---

2 | Taken from Rob Bell's excellent book on suffering, *Drops Like Stars*, p.114-115.
3 | 2 Corinthians 1:3-5

Becoming dangerous in all the right ways is about walking the path of humility, not pursuing the path of self-glorification. This is why you are probably more familiar with the ministries founded by Danny, Clarissa, Bill and Cathy than with these people themselves.

Bill and Cathy are otherwise known as William and Catherine.

In 1865, William Booth was invited to hold a series of evangelistic meetings in the East End of London. He set up a tent in a Quaker graveyard, and his services became an instant success. This proved to be the end of his wanderings as an independent traveling evangelist. His renown as a religious leader spread throughout London, and he attracted followers who were dedicated to fight for the souls of men and women.

Thieves, prostitutes, gamblers, and drunkards were among Booth's first converts to Christianity. To congregations who were desperately poor, he preached hope and salvation. His aim was to lead people to Christ and link them to a church for further spiritual guidance.

Many churches, however, did not accept Booth's followers because of their past. So Booth continued giving his new converts spiritual direction, challenging them to save others like themselves. Soon, they too were preaching and singing in the streets as a living testimony to the power of God.

In 1867, Booth had only 10 full-time workers, but by 1874, the number had grown to 1,000 volunteers and 42 evangelists, all serving under the name "The Christian Mission." Booth assumed the title of general superintendent, with his followers calling him "General." Known as the "Hallelujah Army," the converts spread out of the East End of London into neighboring areas and then to other cities.

Booth was reading a printer's proof of the 1878 annual report when he noticed the statement "The Christian Mission is a volunteer army." Crossing out the words "volunteer army," he penned in "Salvation Army." From those words came the basis of the foundation deed of The Salvation Army.[4]

---

4 | Taken from the website of the Salvation Army.

Clarissa preferred the shorter name Clara. Her last name was Barton. Civil War soldiers just called her "the angel of the battlefield." Perhaps you recognize the fruits of her pain.

Inspired by her experiences ... Barton corresponded with Red Cross officials in Switzerland after her return to the United States. They recognized her leadership abilities for including this country in the global Red Cross network and for influencing the United States government to sign the Geneva Treaty. Armed with a letter from the head of the International Committee of the Red Cross, Barton took her appeal to President Rutherford B. Hayes in 1877, but he looked on the treaty as a possible "entangling alliance" and rejected it. His successor, President James Garfield, was supportive and seemed ready to sign it when he was assassinated. Finally, Garfield's successor, Chester Arthur, signed the treaty in 1882 and a few days later, the Senate ratified it. The Red Cross received its first congressional charter in 1900 ...[5]

Soon after praying to St. Jude Thaddeus, the patron saint of lost causes, Danny Thomas' career as an entertainer and actor took off. However, his Hollywood fame was eventually dwarfed by the legacy he built through what is known today as **St. Jude's Hospital.**

That prayer to St. Jude marked a pivotal moment in his life. Soon after, he began finding work, eventually becoming one of the biggest stars of radio, film and television in his day. And as one of the world's biggest celebrities, Danny used his fame to fulfill his vow to St. Jude Thaddeus and to change the lives of thousands of children and families.

A unique research institution, Danny's shrine to St. Jude Thaddeus was originally to be a general children's hospital located somewhere in the south. Danny's mentor, Cardinal Samuel Stritch, recommended he look to Memphis, Tennessee, the cardinal's hometown.

By 1955, Danny and a group of Memphis businessmen he'd rallied to build the hospital decided it should be more than a general children's hospital. At the time, the survival rate for childhood cancers was 20 percent, and for those with acute

---

5 | Taken from the website of the Salvation Army.

lymphoblastic leukemia (ALL) – the most common form of childhood cancer — only 4 percent of children would live. They believed that St. Jude could help these families with nowhere else to turn. St. Jude would become a unique research institution where the world's best doctors and scientists would work together to cure childhood cancer, sickle cell and other deadly diseases. And for families with children battling these diseases, Danny wanted to remove the burden of treatment costs so they were free to focus on their child.[6]

Pain Inventory

So you see, it is not enough to just ask, *what are my raw materials, what are my resources, and what is my passion?* You must also ask, what is my pain? Remember the words of Frederich Beuchner:

"Calling is where your deep gladness meets the world's deep need."

Taking an honest inventory of your pain is a fundamental part of discerning the world's deep needs – especially needs that you maybe divinely sensitive to, and specifically shaped and resourced to address. Answer the following questions prayerfully and honestly:

Pain: Personal Experience

- Did you experience any physical pain or sickness as you grew that shaped you in some way?
- Did you experience any family relationship pain; loss, rejection, betrayal, divorce, etc. that shaped you?
- Did you experience any pain related to your peers and/ or friends growing up, such as social rejection, betrayal, bullying, etc. that has shaped your ability to make relationships or trust people?
- Did you experience any pain related to failure or disappointment in school, sports, or extra-curricular activities growing up that has shaped your willingness to try things or take risks?

---

6 | Taken from St. Jude's Hospital website.

Pain: Personal Brokenness

- Have you committed any sin in your life that you have learned from and found healing?

- Have you visited pain upon others in your life that you have deep regrets over and that you have either sought or gained forgiveness and reconciliation?

- Have you made mistakes in your life that you would passionately like to help others avoid or work through? Are you comfortable with telling your own personal story of pain and brokenness as a means of encouraging others to open up to healing?

- Are you willing to be humble and model the flow of seeking, giving and receiving forgiveness as it relates to helping other people heal?

Pain: Vicarious Experience

- What pain have you experienced that you would not want anyone else to experience? Have you experienced healing from something that you yourself could help someone else through?

- What things have you witnessed personally that broke your heart?

- What types of things on the news produce an emotional response in your heart? Example: natural disaster, racism, government or business corruption, child abuse or abduction, sex trafficking, abortion, disease and starvation issues, drug addiction, poverty, homelessness, mental illness issues, divorce and family issues, etc.

- If you had the power to change three things in the world what would they be?_____

  _____

  _____

- Are you aware of any non-profit agencies or churches that address the pain and/or issues you wrote down in the previous five questions?

Conclusion: If You Were Paying Attention ...

... you will have noticed that I left out one person from our original list of people who used their pain to make a difference: **April.**

I left out April so that I could emphasize something very important: divine difference-makers come in all shapes and sizes. Not every person will end up starting a world-renown non-profit organization. This does not mean they are not important. In fact, the biblical witness is just the opposite ... God is most pleased with the quiet, behind-the-scenes person who faithfully uses their pain for the sake of the Kingdom. Consider this quiet fab four:

- **Tertius** – the scribe for the Apostle Paul. It is thought that Paul struggled with his eyesight and so he needed faithful and competent scribes to write down his letters. Tertius made possible the majority of what we know today as the New Testament (see Romans 16:22).

- **Priscilla and Aquila** – this quiet couple saw the giftedness and passion of Apollos after hearing him preach. However, they also saw some areas in which Apollos needed to grow. With great tact and love, scripture describes how they quietly pulled Apollos aside and further strengthened him in the doctrine of the faith (see Acts 118:24-26). It is thought in some circles that Apollos would go on to write the New Testament book of Hebrews.

- **Barnabas** – few people know that there was some early strife between Paul and a fellow missionary named Barnabas over the failings of an early follower named John Mark. Paul was reluctant to give John Mark a second chance – but Barnabas opposed Paul, taking John Mark with him on his journeys (see Acts 15:36). In doing so, Barnabas lived up to his name "encourager."

- **Philemon** – even though a book of the New Testament is named after him, Philemon remains a very behind-the-scenes figure. In short, Paul comes into contact with a slave on the run named Onesimus. Onesimus converts to Christianity but fears returning to his owner, Philemon, for fear of reprisal. Philemon is also a convert and Paul writes to encourage Philemon to treat Onesimus not only with mercy, but also as a fellow brother in Christ. Historically, there is evidence that suggests that Philemon took Paul's admonitions to heart, forgiving and freeing Onesimus. This same Onesimus may have gone on to later become the Bishop of Ephesus.[7]

April's story is a modern day behind-the-scenes example of how pain can lead us to our calling. Consider her story taken from her blog entry from May 24, 2016, entitled "Turning Suffering Into Hope":

"By the time I was diagnosed with bipolar disorder I had been through a manic and psychotic episode, traveled across the country, and ended up homeless.

"I was offered help by an organization that provides housing to people with severe and persistent mental illness. I had a tiny room in an apartment with two other roommates. I could barely leave my room, let alone the apartment. I was terrified of catching a life-threatening disease from one of my roommates. I joined a gym so I could take showers in the locker room, which seemed cleaner to me than the bathroom I had to share with these two strangers. (OCD is not exactly logical.) I could hardly look people in the eye when they spoke to me. I rented movies from the library and watched them in my room all day until a hint of twilight fell upon the street outside and I could go to bed without feeling guilty. I spent my food stamps on ice cream and cookies and binged and purged while I watched the movies. I used the bag I had brought the food home in, then snuck it out to the trash outside, praying I wouldn't see my roommates.

"These behaviors and more accompanied me for months while I lived at the program. But eventually I started to feel a little better and after six months I moved out of the residential program into an apartment of my own. I finished my bachelor's degree. My life took several other turns which I've written about previously. But one day I went back to the residential program to say hello to my old counselor. He was delighted to see me and hear about all the things I had accomplished since leaving the program. He offered me a job.

---

7 | *The International Standard Bible Encyclopedia*, Geoffrey W. Bromily, Vol. 3, p.604.

"I was so overcome with joy I hardly knew what to say. I accepted immediately and began working about two weeks later. Now I work with people who are in such similar circumstances to what I went through that I am in awe of the privilege afforded me. All I can do is humble myself and ask for God's blessing as I move through this new phase of my life. The residential program isn't perfect but it provides a way for people who are willing and able to do the work on the road to wellness.

"I wouldn't give up all my suffering for anything, because it means I can now help others who are suffering. I am propelled forward by the words of Thomas à Kempis, who wrote the inimitable My Imitation of Christ in the early 1400's:

" 'Always be ready for battle if you wish for victory; you cannot win the crown of patience without a struggle; if you refuse to suffer, you refuse the crown. Therefore, if you desire the crown, fight manfully and endure patiently. Without labour, no rest is won; without battle, there can be no victory.' "

"I had the phrase, 'Without suffering, there is no crown," tattooed on my arm in Latin, in case I ever forget. Suffering is powerful and suffering can be turned around to help others. Never regret the path you have been sent on."

I once heard a colleague of mine say, "With God, the little things are the big things." I think that is true. Moreover, I think April is a great example of this truth. She doesn't head up a national organization, and yet her service is a big thing.

She has learned to use her pain, not avoid it.
In human terms, she is the blemish in the rug where the Spirit enters.

She has learned to walk with God in her suffering, and in so doing, April Krueger has become dangerous in all the right ways.

You go girl.

Part 3

First Steps

First Step: Divine Feedback

"Write with the door closed, rewrite with the door open."

Stephen King,
"On Writing: A Memoir of the Craft"

During my last year of college my Jazz band director, Al Noice, retired after several decades of service. Studying as a music major, I had spent a lot of time with Al playing in his various bands. In addition, my relationship with him went even further back because I had benefited from his tutelage as a high school student while attending International Music Camp.[1]

When I was asked to share some stories and words of encouragement at his retirement banquet I was honored. I loved the man.

It was a big, black tie event – all of the heavy hitters were present; the college president, various department chairs, and a "who's who" of local music movers and shakers. It turned out to be a rather infamous start to my career as a public communicator. As my moment to speak arrived, I strode to the podium to share about 10 minutes worth of material. About five minutes into the tribute, the audience reaction seemed to affirm everything I was hoping to accomplish:

I was killing it.

The room seemed to respond to my every word, laughing at my stories, even to the point where I was surprised. Satisfied that I had done my job, I confidently walked back to my seat, the crowd still seemingly following me with their eyes. That should have been my first warning ...

When I sat down, I instinctively relaxed, crossing my legs. That's when one of my classmates, with a subtle whisper, opened my eyes. That's when the truth, in all its cold, horrifying glory, hit me ...

---

1 | International Music Camp is located at the U.S. / Canadian border in between North Dakota and Manitoba. The camp itself is part of the International Peace Gardens.

"Dude, your fly is open."

Now, that didn't necessarily have to be an issue – after all, many times, men catch themselves with their fly open before anyone notices. I only wish that would've been the case with me. As my mind frantically factored in the context, I quickly realized that it wasn't my eloquence the audience was captivated by, but my wardrobe malfunction. Any hope that they didn't notice was quickly melted away by the facts:

• The speaking podium I stood behind would've normally blocked the distracting view. But in this case, the podium was a tall, beautiful, transparent glass specimen.

• Often when the fly is open, it isn't noticed because the pants, shirt (if tucked in) and/or underwear are similar in color. Not only was this not true with me – it was amplified by the black tie occasion. I was wearing black pants, with a white dress shirt tucked in … and the tail of the shirt was conspicuously sticking out of the opening – as if my wardrobe was secretly playing a capricious game of hide and seek with the audience.

Yikes ….

As we take the stage in our lives, the world will always offer us two kinds of feedback – the kind we think is real, and the kind that is real. If we are honest, we must admit that it is easy to misinterpret reality, misreading the general feedback from the world. The truth is, we all need that person who loves us enough to say "dude your fly is open."

Often people think the hardest part about authoring a book is the actual writing process. I think most writers would disagree. The hardest part is the step after the writing process – the editing process. It is in this step that you expose your work to someone else for the first time for his or her feedback, criticism, and corrections. It is very scary, but it is an absolutely necessary part of creating a good book. Stephen King was correct when he said, "Write with the door closed, rewrite with the door open."

As we partner with our creator to write the story of our lives, seeking to discern our calling and gifts, we must be open to letting others participate in the process. It is scary, at times heartbreaking, but a non-negotiable if we are to truly honor God with our potential.

Over the past 13 chapters, not only you have explored the biblical nature of calling and spiritual gifting, but you have also taken the time to discern your raw material, resources, passion and pain. Now it is time to let others in on your story, giving them the power to affirm, adjust, or otherwise bring a reality check into your observations.

Everyone Needs Feedback

We often forget that no one is exempt from the need for feedback. No one is capable of fully discerning his or her calling with complete objectivity. That's ok. God created us not only to be gifted, but also to discover and exercise these gifts in community. God delights in his children loving and supporting each other. He desires that his goodness not simply come through his personal activity, but even more so, through the activity of his children as they love and serve each other.

Perhaps one the most striking and beautiful examples of this is the Amish barn-raising. This activity is still quite common today, and it is an inspiring picture of the how a loving community not only serves each other, but also **develops and refines the gifts of its members in the process.**

In May of 2014, Scott Miller obtained permission to record one of these Amish events, but only with the condition that he also participate in the work. This condition wasn't insisted upon because the Amish community was in need of workers. Rather, as Miller would put it, it was insisted upon so that he could fully immerse himself in the *koinonia*[2] of the phenomena.

> " ... *while all you see in the video are men, an Amish barn-raising is actually an all-hands-on-deck affair. Attendance is mandatory in the community, though the Amish don't view "mandatory" as the pejorative we selfish Americans do: "We enjoy barn-raisings," an Amish farmer told writer Gene Logsdon*

---

2 | Koinonia is a Greek word found in the New Testament used to describe the unique sense of community characterized by the early church. A good working definition of koinonia would be "bonds forged through a shared sense of service, sacrifice, purpose and vision."

in 1983. "So many come to work that no one has to work very hard. And we get in a good visit."

That's because to the Amish, a barn-raising falls into the category of activity known as a "frolic," a combination of group labor and social mixing, which builds and solidifies the community as surely as it does the barn. All able-bodied members of the settlement are in attendance, meaning there can be more than a hundred families on hand, and with Amish families averaging eight children each, you can do the math.

All have a role to play, regardless of age and gender. The younger, more able-bodied men are the ones you see clambering up and down the structure. The older men whose climbing days are behind them stay down below, passing up supplies, and the most experienced serve as foremen. The entire building operation is "typically led by one or two master Amish 'engineers,' who lay out plans for the barn and assure the materials are available," according to Amish America.

The community's women are also on-site, preparing the gargantuan feast and snacks required to feed this mass gathering, while girls carry the plates out at mealtime, ferry juice jugs, and assist with the cleaning up.

Boys not yet old enough to participate are put to lesser tasks like fetching tools or de-nailing old boards that will be re-used, while the youngest boys are on hand to watch and learn. By the time an Amish boy has grown to a man he has observed every stage of multiple barn-raisings, has learned the tools and now has the education needed to effectively pitch in. "They like to work with wood, and they learn the niceties of barn-building at an early age," wrote Helen Forrest McKee in a 1978 article on the phenomenon. And among the children "There is no fighting or crying and no need for an adult to supervise them."

In Amish community, each of its members is nurtured to serve, and in the process to have his or her gifts recognized, developed and honed for the benefit of those around them.

Does this sound familiar? (**Hint:** The Apostle Paul wrote about this to the baby believers in the Corinthian church.)

The Amish actually have the audacity to take the Bible literally when it says,

> *"There are different kinds of gifts, but the same Spirit distributes them. There are different kinds of service, but the same Lord. There are different kinds of working, but in all of them and in everyone it is the same God at work. Now to each one the manifestation of the Spirit is given for the common good."*[3]

Indeed, we see several examples of how godly feedback and mentoring benefited people in the stories of scripture:

- In the book of Esther, God positions a beautiful young Jewish girl named Hadassah (later named Esther) as queen of Persia just as an evil man named Haman plots to eliminate her people. Esther is young, unconfident, and hesitant about approaching the king uninvited. Esther's uncle, Mordecai, helps her to see that her position and beauty are not mere happenstance, but gifts from God given in order that she might save her people: **"Do not think that because you are in the king's house you alone of all the Jews will escape. For if you remain silent at this time, relief and deliverance for the Jews will arise from another place, but you and your father's family will perish. And who knows but that you have come to your royal position for such a time as this?"**[4]

- A young man named Apollos emerges on the scene as the early church is growing. Apollos is passionate and articulate, but his knowledge of the Gospel is incomplete. Fortunately for him, a Christian couple named Priscilla and Aquila overhear him, see his gifting and potential, and quietly pull him aside for further instruction. **"He began to speak boldly in the synagogue, but when Priscilla and Aquila heard him, they took him aside and explained to him the way of God more accurately."**[5] Their mentorship and willingness to bring correction to Apollos benefits not only the church at that time, but in the millennia to come as it is widely believed that Apollos authored the New Testament book of Hebrews.

- Timothy has been left in charge of the church in Ephesus. During the course of numerous missionary journeys, the Apostle

---

3 | 1 Corinthians 12:4-7
4 | Esther 4:12-14
5 | Acts 18:26

Paul has mentored Timothy. And yet, we have evidence that Timothy still struggles with timidity and a general lack of confidence. Left in isolation, he may well have faded into irrelevance. But Timothy has a secret weapon – two amazing women – his grandmother Lois, and his mother Eunice. Together they support and gird Timothy in his ministry, helping to nurture and release more fully his giftedness. In a letter of encouragement to Timothy, Paul would write, **"I thank God, whom I serve, as my ancestors did, with a clear conscience, as night and day I constantly remember you in my prayers. Recalling your tears, I long to see you, so that I may be filled with joy. I am reminded of your sincere faith, which first lived in your grandmother Lois and in your mother Eunice and, I am persuaded, now lives in you also. For this reason I remind you to fan into flame the gift of God, which is in you through the laying on of my hands. For the Spirit God gave us does not make us timid, but gives us power, love and self-discipline."**

So, we see that feedback is not something we experience as merely a corrective when we get things wrong, but is something that God has designed as part of the process so that a person's giftedness might eventually serve the community to its fullest extent.

But this begs the question – who should you ask for feedback, and what should you ask them? Well, let's explore that ...

Who To Ask

The answer to the question, "who should you ask" is simple, but not easy. It's simple because the quality is self-evident, it's not easy because it is hard to find.

Who should you ask?
Ask people in your life who will be honest with you.

I know ... not exactly rocket science. However, it is a challenge to find those people. This is because people are dishonest for many reasons – and often those reasons are born of affection. This is why many times asking a family member for feedback in this area may not necessarily be helpful. They love you and don't want to say things that might hurt you – even if they are true. How many disillusioned singers on American Idol believed they were good because "mom always told me I'm destined to be a star." What mom wouldn't want that for their child? OK .. you get my point – right?

The most helpful people will be those who are capable of being honest with you – even if hurts. So ... who is that for you?

One way of discerning that is to think about people from your past who have already demonstrated that quality. Looking back over my own life, the following people come to mind:

- My mom and dad (Yes, they are capable of being honest with me – but remember, many are not.)
- A couple of basketball coaches
- A couple of pastors
- Three band directors
- My brothers and my brother-in-law
- My wife
- Three of my work colleagues
- A close personal friend

These are people who have already demonstrated in my life the ability to tell me truthful things – whether they are pleasant or difficult to hear. They are also people who have remained in relationship with me (when possible) through good and bad times. Many are elders. Several are people who have experience in the directions I was exploring. They are people also who believe in me – even with the knowledge of my faults.

So ... once again, we are looking for people who are capable of telling you the truth, and:

- Have been a consistent part of your life
- Have an abundance of life experience
- Have spiritual maturity
- Have experience in the areas you are feeling drawn toward

- Gain no personal benefits from counseling you one way or another
- Know your faults – but still believe in you

Remember – no one person has to embody all of the above criteria. However, the collection of people from whom you get feedback should reflect the list above.

With that in mind, take a moment to pray and ask the Lord for guidance, asking Him to speak through the people he draws to you in this process.

Now – start your list:

_____   _____

_____   _____

_____   _____

What to Ask

What you ask if just as important as who you ask. Remember, your goal is to discern the most truthful picture of how God shaped you – your raw material, your resources, your passion and your pain. The people you bring into this process for feedback should help you in affirming where you are seeing these things accurately, and where you might have some blind spots.

I recommend the following questions as a starting point:

In each of these assessment areas:

- What have I written down that you agree with – that you see as accurate?
- What have I written down that you disagree with – that you see as inaccurate?
- What have I written down that seems incomplete or not fully flushed out?
- Do you see anything that suggests I'm not being honest about myself?

- Have I inflated any observations about myself?

- Have I undervalued any observations about myself?

- Have I omitted anything about my raw material, resources or pain that I should think about?

- Am I being realistic about how I see my passions or how I might use them?

- Have you observed me blessing people in any activities or ways that I have not written down in this assessment?

- Have you observed me blessing people in any activities or ways consistent with what I noted in this assessment?

- Do you think what I have written down in this assessment can lead me to a full-time vocation – or would it be better to practice these gifts and passions as a side pursuit?

- Can you think of any first-steps or opportunities where I can further explore what I have written down on this assessment?

- In what ways might I need to mature in character in order to more fully live and work within my potential calling?

These questions should get the ball rolling in terms of flushing out more fully the truth about how God shaped you. By all means, do not limit the discussion to these questions, but let them act as the starting point. I recommend you write down any helpful observations, refining your worksheet as you go. Remember – not everything you hear may be pleasant. You might hear some things that surprise you. You will also hear some things that are encouraging. Throughout this process continue in prayer to the Lord, asking Him to teach and prepare you. Remaining humble and teachable throughout this process will be your greatest asset.

Conclusion: Your Destination
Leads To Your Road

As of August 15, 2016, I will have been in the full-time ministry for 25 years, the last 12 as a pastor.

And yet growing up I never wanted to be a pastor …

... a pro-football player? Yes (2nd grade). A marine biologist? Yes (4th grade). A lawyer or doctor? Yes (high school). A music writer and producer? Yes (college) ...

... but never a pastor. I mean, seriously – who would want to be on their best behavior for that long? And yet God had other plans.

My pastor during my teen years was man named Jay Stratton. He was a great man. He somehow was able to combine reverence, authority, and gentility as a pastor in ways I have never been able to approach. He and I got along pretty well. However, during those years we did have one ongoing disagreement – my vocation. When Jay looked at me he did not see a professional athlete, a biologist, a doctor, lawyer or music producer.

What he did see was a pastor ... and I hated it.

Twice during my teen years he visited with me about my vocation. Both times he would lean back in his office chair, light up his pipe – I still love the smell of pipe tobacco today – and weave the conversation toward "my calling." I thought the idea was ridiculous. I actually laughed in his face the second time. As I would later say to someone else later in life, "I have better things to do with my time."

I could be such an arrogant little turd.

Interestingly enough, Pastor Jay never discouraged me from pursuing my dreams, my ideas of what I was supposed to be. And in retrospect, I can see why now.

When God is calling someone
it isn't the road that leads to the destination –
it's the destination that leads to the road.

Sound backward?

It sounds backward – but in God's plan it is true.

You see, what I didn't tell you is that Jay promised to bless me in my pursuits as long as I was willing to be open to what God desired. Not fully understanding the implications of that, I agreed, even though in my heart it was still very much about me, and what I wanted.

But you know what they say ...

Give God an inch, and He will take ... a lifetime.

Even as I pursued my dream of being a big shot in the music industry, God was working – in me and around me. You see, being a music producer wasn't my destination – it was my road. It was the path I needed to travel in order to discern my strengths, my weaknesses, my true passions, and what was really important in life. Through trial and error, experience, frustration and self-discovery I discovered that there was a difference between what I envisioned myself doing, and what God had positioned me to do.

A year into pursuing my "dream," I was on a plane flying back to Nashville, Tenn., when suddenly I just knew ... I knew what God wanted me to do ... what He wanted me to be ...

That night I traded in my happiness for God's joy.
It was the best trade ever.

Two years later I found myself sitting in a booth at a local restaurant buying lunch for Pastor Jay Stratton. He had just been diagnosed with cancer and it didn't look promising. I knew the clock was ticking, and there was something I needed to say.

"You were right and I was wrong," I said. "You saw something in me that I didn't see in myself. Something I didn't want to see. Thanks for taking the chance to tell me the truth. Forgive my response – I was young and prideful."

Jay just looked at me, nodding and smiling. He no longer smoked his pipe, but his clothes still smelled faintly of tobacco.

I continued, "I thought it was a joke – you telling me to be a pastor. Well ... I guess the joke is on me."

Jay took a sip of his diet Coke, and then he leaned into the table while folding his hands together.

"It was just a hunch," he said, smiling through his pepper-gray mustache, "but I've learned to pay attention to those hunches. God has way of speaking through them. Life can be funny ... but your calling, Randy, is no joke. I'm very proud of you."

The same is true for you.

Life is funny, but your calling is no joke.

God wants to speak to you – and He will do it through others if you let Him. They may tell you what you don't want to hear. They may steer you in surprising directions. They may even tell you in some symbolic way that *your fly is down.* But if you are humble enough to listen, you might discover that just when you thought you were looking for your destination, you discovered your road.

May you be so blessed.

First Steps:
Divine Divergences

"Calling is connection: Uncovering our calling is a deliberate choice to serve others and to make a difference in the world. Our calling is made manifest in service to others ..."

David Shapiro, "Work Reimagined: Uncover Your Calling"

In general, I was a pretty good student in school. I mostly got A's and B's. But it is probably safe to say that, at least early on, I was more book-smart than world-smart. In my middle school years, this was most clearly demonstrated by my grades in the "hands-on" classes – namely Woodshop, and Home Economics. Those two classes revealed my weaknesses. I got a "C" in both, and I was lucky it wasn't worse.

I remember one specific assignment in Home Economics that will serve to illustrate my main point in this chapter. The task was to go home, and using a recipe provided by the teacher, make a batch of sugar cookies. I know, I know ... just plain sugar cookies. This wasn't exactly an Iron Chef challenge. In fact it was about as simple a recipe as one could hope to draw in the universe of the culinary cookie cookbook. I remember thinking I just might have half a chance at securing a "B" ...

Well ... I got a "B".
That is, if "B" stands for bad.

My olfactory memory can still faintly recall the aroma of my sugar cookies as they were baking in my mother's olive green oven. They smelled good. My heart was filled with hope. As the timer "dinged" with a certain kind of chirpy optimism, I donned my oven mitts and pulled the sheet of cookies out for inspection. The color was good, light brown with slightly darker edges. They were the right size and firmness. But something wasn't quite right – they didn't quite have the 'sheen' that appeared in the recipe picture. After waiting the prescribed three minutes, I gently freed one with a spatula and took a bite.

It wasn't bad ... but it wasn't a cookie.
It was a biscuit.

I still remember my mother talking through the recipe with me ...
"Flour?"
"Check."

"Baking powder?"
"Check."

"Butter?"
"Check."

"Sugar?"

(Silence)

"Sugar?"

"Ummmmmm ....."

I'll never forget the look my mother gave me as I sat there in silence – unable to confirm her query. It was that look that only mother's can give – an incredulous and forlorn face betraying a mix of emotions. It was as if her countenance was simultaneously saying *"You poor boy"* and *"My teenage son has brain damage."*

That's right.
I made sugar cookies ... without the sugar.

I think when it comes to discerning and pursuing our calling and spiritual gifts, we often make the same mistake. We often miss a key ingredient in the recipe.

All Ingredients Matter

In the previous chapters you engaged in an honest assessment of your raw material, resources, passion and pain. You sat with trusted friends and advisors and sifted through your observations for those that were most true to who you are. Now comes the time to see how each of these areas can contribute to discerning your calling and direction – much like all the ingredients are important to a good recipe.

As much as possible, we want to avoid leaving any of the key ingredients out. We don't want to try to make sugar cookies without the sugar. If we ignore raw material – we are bound for frustration and feelings of inadequacy. If we leave out potential resources, we may struggle to see how the road can lay before us. If we shrink back from including our passion, we may settle for lives of security rather than significance. If we fail to consider our pain, we may pursue our gifting in narcissistic ways that put self-fulfillment above the needs around us.[1]

You've probably noticed I'm a fan of John Ortberg's writing. In his previously quoted book, *If You Want to Walk On Water, You've Got To Get Out of the Boat*, he tells the story of his friend Bob Buford, and how important it is to consider all the ingredients of one's shape.

> *"When I think of the value of receiving discernment from more than one person, from a 'clearness committee,' I think of Bob Buford. Bob was an immensely successful television tycoon who sensed God was calling him to get out of a very well-appointed boat. In the words of his book, Halftime, he wanted to move from 'success to significance.' He and his wife, Linda, met at length with one adviser, who helped him clarify his sense of purpose immensely. Then this adviser suggested a questionable next step: 'Sell your company and invest in the ministry-oriented projects you've been talking about.' Bob writes,*

> *" 'I sat there, stunned by the implications of this decision. Linda appeared no less stunned. I could almost see the stereotypical images of ministers, missionaries, and monastics passing through her mind. Would we be a philanthropic couple passing out money until our sack was empty? Would we be required to dress like a minister and his spouse?'*

> *"Bob goes on to explain how he assembled his own clearness committee (though he didn't use that language). Together they helped him see that what he loves most and does best involves strategic thinking and organizational leadership. They discerned that if he were to sell his company, he would lose a platform that could be leveraged for a great deal of good. Instead, they helped him see that his passions and*

---

1 | Remember Frederich Buechner's quote, *"Your calling is where your deep gladness meets the world's deep needs"* (paraphrased).

competencies were ideally suited to help pastors and church leaders deal with issues of organizational complexity and mission effectiveness. Today he leads a ministry that develops leadership for key churches throughout the country – and loves doing it. But if he had run out and followed his first adviser's counsel – if he had sold his business and simply doled out the funds – he never would have experienced the effectiveness or fulfillment that he has today."

This is the wisdom of gathering multiple advisors. Not everyone can see everything – including you! Bob's effectiveness would've been vastly underutilized had he been reduced to merely a source of money. His capital was much more diverse than just cash – he had a vast pool of knowledge and experience to share. Had he followed the more traditional path initially suggested, key ingredients of Bob's gift mix would've been ignored, and many churches and organizations would've lost out on invaluable guidance.

This is why this chapter is entitled "Divine Divergences." What we are looking for are places where your raw material, resources, passion, and pain intersect. It is in these intersection points that your calling lies. Bob Buford could've chosen simple philanthropy, but it was not a Divine Divergence point for him. Bob's money wasn't the most valuable thing he had to give – rather his money would free him to travel and give away the most valuable thing. Philanthropy ignored the Resource portion of his gift mix – it ignored all of the knowledge and experience he had to offer.

Finding Help in Discerning Your Divine Divergences

Bob Buford aptly illustrated the first of three resources when it comes to unveiling the intersection points in your gift mix.

1. Trusted Friends – The same friends that helped you sift out the truth of your gift mix can also be helpful in discerning where intersections might exist. Bob's friends effectively reminded him of his most valuable gift, and then helped steer him towards sharing that in a way that was much more consistent with his raw material and passion. His significance was found in service to the Kingdom of God not as a philanthropist, but as a consultant. Asking your friends the following questions may open your eyes to possibilities you haven't been aware of or considered:

- Does anything listed and affirmed in my assessment stand out to you? If so, why?
- Am I underutilizing any aspects of my gift mix?
- Have I underestimated any resources that might help me move closer toward serving in my gift mix?
- Have I been blind or resistant to opportunities to exercise my gifts or work in my passions?
- Are you aware of any jobs or vocational areas where I might serve more joyfully and fully in my gift mix?
- Are you aware of needs in the community that my gifts might effectively address?
- Are there any entrepreneurial possibilities I should consider that might unleash my gifts more fully in service to those around me?

2. Experts and Professionals in Related Fields – This is one of the most important areas to explore as you seek to discern intersection points and possible directions. Taking the time to speak with people who are working in your potential fields of giftedness will:

- Yield extremely important information
- Reveal any misperceptions you may have
- Uncover options and possibilities you may not realize exist
- Bring clarity to the long term path and immediate steps you may need to take

My wife, Pam, has been working increasingly in her area of giftedness for the past eight years through her non-profit organization, Providence Ranch Ministries. However, she didn't just jump into running an independent 501-c3 organization. She took baby steps ... patiently.

One of those important baby steps involved entering into a mentoring relationship with Crystal Peaks Youth Ranch. Crystal

Peaks is lead by Troy and Kim Meeder and is a nationally known example of the kind of horse-based, mentoring ministry Pam was feeling called toward. We were fortunate enough to connect with them during a local visit to Bismarck, and to participate in their new ministry training seminar. Through this connection, Pam and I were able to learn many things as painlessly as possible that allowed us to get Providence Ranch Ministries started on the right foot. We learned invaluable information about structure, governance, programming, fund-raising philosophy, and how to patiently start small and allow the organization to grow in God's time. Our connection continues today, and we continue to benefit from the mentoring example Crystal Peaks offers.

Meeting with people in this way requires the willingness to engage in research and take initiative. It also requires a special kind of humility and vulnerability – a willingness to learn, and be open to doing things the right way, not the quick way. It is possible, for example, these professionals might suggest you get further training or education. They may prescribe a path that will take longer than you previously envisioned. You must remain open about how God wants to shape you in this process.

Below is a sampling of questions you might find helpful to ask when engaged in this stage:

- What aspects of your work give you energy and fulfill you?
- Are there aspects of your work, perhaps not as obvious to people, that you find frustrating?
- (After sharing your gift mix assessment with them) In what ways is my gift mix a match for this work? In what ways is it not?
- Are there skills, education or training that I may need to attain in order to enter into this field?
- What moral challenges are present in your work?
- Are there some other related jobs in this field that I may want to consider?
- Are there other related fields that I may want to investigate?
- Given the season of life I am in – are there any personal considerations or timing issues I should consider before moving further in this field?

3. Internet Research – Today we have a big advantage when it comes to researching just about any topic. The advent of the Internet and worldwide web has revolutionized our access to information in terms of speed, breadth, and depth. Through the Internet we have access to the best libraries, the most respected newspaper archives, the top scholars, and most up-to-date research. The Internet has vastly reduced the negative effect of geography, making the world a much smaller and more accessible place.

For example, do you remember my son Josh, the Custer House tour guide? Just the other day we were discussing the state and national park systems as potential calling/career tracks. It's one thing to enjoy a job as a local tour guide in an entry-level position, but what about the long-term prospects? With that question in mind, we conducted an Internet search using as key words the areas Josh was passionate about and naturally good at; history, outdoors, drama, teaching, national parks.

Do you know what popped up? Well … actually quite a few things, but among them was an intriguing possibility; Park Historian, National Park System. Within two clicks of the mouse we were immersed into everything you wanted to know about what a park historian did, what skills were needed, what education and training was involved, what the pay scale was, where jobs were available, etc. Moreover, links to the email addresses of current park historians at various national parks were also available.

Not only could Josh learn about details and pathways for this job, but he could also quickly and easily contact actual park historians – making the task of contacting people in the potential field of vocation all the easier.

Used correctly, the Internet is an amazing Divine Divergence search engine and networking tool! Research that used to be nearly impossible, or at best time consuming, is now readily available to anyone with a willingness to do the work.

Take a look at your assessment. What key words did you write down in your raw materials, resource, passion, and pain sections? Try typing those words into an Internet search engine and start researching where they take you.

I'm not kidding.

Take 20 minutes and do a search of your key words ... now.

I'll wait ... (cue quiet elevator music).

Ok ... back now?

Chances are you have stumbled into some interesting Divine Divergences. Oh ... it may have taken a few different combinations of key words, and a few clicks here and there ... but if you persevered you probably unearthed some helpful information and possibilities.

Now ... if you combine this research with some good, honest conversations with friends and people of experience you should be starting to get somewhere. However some questions still remain ...

What if I am afraid to move forward?

Should I pursue my calling full-time or part-time?

How can I serve God and my church better through this information?

And the one question some of you may be entertaining but are afraid to ask ...

What if I have done all this reading, research and work and it still isn't clear to me where to start? Am I a lost cause?

Well ... don't despair. You are not a lost cause.
There is always a next step with God.

Follow me to our final chapter ...

First Steps: Divine Action

"Do stuff. Be clenched, curious. Not waiting for inspiration's shove or society's kiss on your forehead. Pay attention. It's all about paying attention. Attention is vitality. It connects you with others. It makes you eager. Stay eager."

Susan Sontag

His father was a deacon of the church.

While still a young teenager, he was kidnapped and taken to Ireland. Enslaved, he lived a dangerous life among the Celts as a shepherd. Through his suffering, he drew closer to God. He would later write:

> *"The love of God and his fear grew in me more and more, as did the faith, and my soul was rosed (sic), so that, in a single day, I have said as many as a hundred prayers and in the night, nearly the same. I prayed in the woods and on the mountain, even before dawn. I felt no hurt from the snow or ice or rain."* [1]

After six long years, he is told by God in a dream to escape to the coast where he miraculously found a boat, and made it back home.

Whew ... he made it.... right?

Not so fast. God wasn't done.

After many years, the former slave, now a cleric in the church, received a second dream.

> *"I saw a man coming, as it were from Ireland. His name was Victoricus, and he carried many letters, and he gave me one of them. I read the heading: 'The Voice of the Irish.' As I began the letter, I imagined in that moment that I heard the voice of those very people who were near the wood of Foclut, which is*

---

1 | From St. Patrick's memoir *The Confession.*

beside the western sea – and they cried out, as with one voice: 'We appeal to you, holy servant boy, to come and walk among us.' "

Despite the immense danger, he eventually obeyed the dream and returned to the land of his bondage. With his life constantly under threat, he endeavored to share the Gospel, ultimately starting several monasteries, converting thousands, and translating the Latin Bible into the native Celt language. He is also connected to the legends of driving the snakes out of Ireland as well as using the three-leaf clover to illustrate the Holy Trinity.

And to think that today this man's legacy is associated with green beer, a parade, and a day of general drunkenness.

Yes ... we are talking about St. Patrick.
A man of faith. A man of action.

In Isaiah, Chapter 6, we see God at work in a similar way. A wayward Israel needs to hear the word of the LORD, and Isaiah hears the call:

In the year that King Uzziah died, I saw the Lord, high and exalted, seated on a throne; and the train of his robe filled the temple. Above him were seraphim, each with six wings: With two wings they covered their faces, with two they covered their feet, and with two they were flying. And they were calling to one another:

"Holy, holy, holy is the Lord Almighty;
the whole earth is full of his glory."

At the sound of their voices the doorposts and thresholds shook and the temple was filled with smoke.

"Woe to me!" I cried. "I am ruined! For I am a man of unclean lips, and I live among a people of unclean lips, and my eyes have seen the King, the Lord Almighty."

Then one of the seraphim flew to me with a live coal in his hand, which he had taken with tongs from the altar. With it he touched my mouth and said, "See, this has touched your lips; your guilt is taken away and your sin atoned for."

*Then I heard the voice of the Lord saying, "Whom shall I send?
And who will go for us?"*

And I said, "Here am I. Send me!"

*He said, "Go and tell this people:
" 'Be ever hearing, but never understanding;
be ever seeing, but never perceiving.'*

*Make the heart of this people calloused;
make their ears dull
and close their eyes.
Otherwise they might see with their eyes,
hear with their ears,
understand with their hearts,
and turn and be healed."*

Isaiah wasn't perfect by any means. But once again, he was a man of faith – a man of action.

Faith without action isn't faith at all. James, the brother of Jesus and leader of the early church in Jerusalem would write:

What good is it, my brothers and sisters, if someone claims to have faith but has no deeds? Can such faith save them? Suppose a brother or a sister is without clothes and daily food. If one of you says to them, "Go in peace; keep warm and well fed," but does nothing about their physical needs, what good is it? In the same way, faith by itself, if it is not accompanied by action, is dead.[2]

James is not suggesting that we are saved by our actions, but rather that our actions are evidence of an authentic and living faith. Reformer Martin Luther put it this way:

*"We are saved by faith alone,
but the faith that saves is never alone ..."[3]*

Luther's namesake, a modern day reformer named Martin Luther King Jr., also noted the urgency of action in a broken world when he said:

---

2 | James 2:14-17
3 | *Bondage of the Will.* Luther was no fan of the epistle of James, calling it the "epistle of straw." However, there is harmony in their understanding of the relationship between faith and works.

"I am in Birmingham because injustice is here. Just as the prophets of the eighth century B.C. left their villages and carried their' thus saith the Lord 'far beyond the boundaries of their home towns, and just as the Apostle Paul left his village of Tarsus and carried the gospel of Jesus Christ to the far corners of the Greco Roman world, so am I compelled to carry the gospel of freedom beyond my own home town."[4]

And so here we are.
Your reading is concluding.
Your time for action has come.
Your faith is waiting to catch fire, to answer God's call upon your life with the words, "Send me."

What is your next step? At this point you will find yourself in one of four different places:

- You have a clear idea of what direction to go, but there are few actual job prospects. Vocationally speaking, this is the **Entrepreneurial Path.**

- You have a clear idea of what direction to go AND there are actual job possibilities in existence. This could be either part time or full time. Vocationally speaking, this is the **Established Path.**

- You have a clear idea of what direction to go, but you are in a season of life or a circumstance that necessitates you pursuing this direction part-time alongside your current job or responsibilities. Vocationally speaking, this is the **Extra-Curricular Path.**

- You have taken the assessment but still are unclear about God's direction for your life. Don't despair! ☺ Vocationally speaking, this is the **Explorer Path.**

Which direction you take will depend upon which of these four categories you most identify with. Going forward you are not required to read the categories that don't apply to you. If you are unsure about which one fits you, then it may be helpful to read all of them for further clarity.

---

4 | From King's "Letter From A Birmingham Jail."

The Entrepreneurial Path

Two roads diverged in a wood, and I -
I took the one less traveled by,
And that has made all the difference.

The Road Not Taken, Robert Frost

At this point no matter which road you choose it will constitute "the road less traveled." Following the calling of God, over and above that of the world around us, is always the less traveled path. It is also always the most rewarding.

If you have completed the assessment process, and been fortunate enough to be able to identify some specific directions, you are probably feeling a combination of excitement and apprehension. That's OK. It is a wonderful yet sobering thing to realize with specificity the direction God is calling you toward. Your next steps will be based upon this clarity.

The Entrepreneurial Path is the path of the courageous adventurer. It will require vision, creativity and plain old guts. The rewards, however, are significant.

I remember many years ago my brother, Bob, called me into a meeting at his place of work. Bob was the vice-principle of a local Christian school. It was a good job, but he was feeling restless.

"I need your counsel on a big decision," Bob said. "I'm thinking of resigning my position and launching out on my own full time with Cross Training."

FYI: Cross Training was a basketball camp that Bob and I had started about three years earlier. It was motivated by the desire to instill in kids a healthy balance between good sportsmanship and being competitive. A crazy combination of games, skits, Bible study and basketball instruction, Cross Training had grown from one camp of 80 kids, to several camps of about 400 kids.[5] Truth be told – it was the perfect fit for Bob's gift mix.[6]

---

5 | I was an All-Conference Junior College basketball player. Bob was an All-American college basketball player. Our reputation in the community as both athletes and men of faith empowered the launching of Cross Training.

6 | For more information, visit the website at crosstrainingcamp.com.

My response to Bob's question was actually pretty simple. It was based upon my own experience as a pastor, husband and father.

"Well ... you're newly married but you don't have any kids yet. Once you have little ones your priorities, time availability, and energy levels will change. It will take a lot of work to build Cross Training up to a full time calling – but I think the timing is right, and I think you can do it. But if you are going to do it, do it now. It won't get easier once you and Shaunna have kids."

I know, I know ... thank you Captain Obvious.

Keep this in mind though – when faithful risk is involved, the obvious isn't always so obvious. We need others to speak encouragement, vision and movement into our calling.

Today Cross Training camps constitute the largest sports camp organization in the state of North Dakota, reaching over 1000 kids per season over a range of several sports, leadership training, and Christian mission trips. In addition, Bob shares the Gospel nationally and internationally as a sought-after motivational speaker. Bob took into account the need, his gifting, the timing, and his faith and created his vocation. This is the Entrepreneurial Path.

This path will require every ounce of courage, creativity, wisdom, resources, and faith you can muster – but the impact for the Kingdom of God has tremendous potential.

NEXT STEP:
Prayerfully develop a plan. Get wise counsel. Network vigorously. Launch with laser-focus and build with patience.

The Established Path

This path is pretty straightforward. Vocational opportunities in the Established Path have already been developed in response to needs. This is good news for anyone who identifies him or herself with this category, as it gives you the opportunity to do ample research prior to moving forward.

Certain questions should be entertained when contemplating this path:

- Will you start out pursuing this part-time or full-time?
- Are you willing to relocate in order to take advantage of the best opportunity?
- Are you willing to undergo further training or education in order to prepare yourself?
- What financial considerations are at play? (You may have to take a pay cut necessitating an adjustment of lifestyle)
- Are you humble enough to start at the bottom of the ladder and work your way up?
- How might this change of vocation affect your family?
- Are you prepared to endure the "stink eye" from friends, work colleagues, and family who might not initially understand your change of vocation?
- Do you understand that even if you are in your divine sweet spot that it will not always be easy? Serving God is never easy.

One of the best examples of the Established Path that I can think of is my good friend Bob Peske. Bob is a guitarist extraordinaire, and changed vocations from high school band director to worship director mid-stream in his life. He was loved by his students, appreciated by their parents, and well respected by his colleagues.

And then 20 years into his career, his *calling* came knocking …

After a one-hour meeting with the church council president, Bob found himself in the fetal position in his living room (remember Rich Stearns?) struggling with an excruciating choice between what he thought he wanted to do with his life, and what God wanted him to do. He would later tell me:

"I was in tears. The decision was excruciating. What about my finances? What would my colleagues say? … So many unanswered questions. I prayed feverishly. I knew I was serving God as a band director, but I had the unmistakable sense He wanted me to serve him differently for a season. And then it happened. In a quiet moment when I felt my weakest, God

spoke to me. His presence and voice washed over in release as He said,

"You have no idea how big I am?"

Isn't that the truth?

Bob Peske would go on to serve Charity Lutheran Church for a decade. Eventually he would go back to the public school system and continue serving as band director – but not before God used him to elevate Charity's worship, adult volunteer, and family ministries to the next level. Even today, Bob continues to serve as beloved worship leader part-time. His imprint on the Kingdom of God in the Bismarck area goes without question.

The Established Path is simpler than the others, but it is not easy. It often requires difficult decisions that challenge our financial and social comfort zones. It may require us to humbly embrace a new season of learning. However, in the process not only will you serve God, you will discover over and over again just how big God is. You will see His providence in your life, feel His presence in your service, see His face in those you serve, and be inspired by the scope of his Kingdom.

NEXT STEP:
Pray and research the existing opportunities.
Determine which might fit you best. Weigh the costs,
then move forward with wisdom.

The Extra-Curricular Path

Those who choose the Extra-Curricular Path are the quiet super-heroes of this world. Well ... sometimes not so quiet too. Either way – they are super heroes because they have found a way to pursue their calling while continuing to honor prior commitments.

These are the people who find themselves in a season of life that does not allow them to make full-time commitments because they already have full-time responsibilities. It could be a mother who is raising her children and works part time to contribute to the family income, or the father whose job provides the family with stability.

It could be the retiree who balances being a grandparent with a calling toward meeting a local need, or the business owner who wants to serve in other areas but feels a responsibility towards his or her employees. Anyway ... you get the point.

These people need not be disqualified from pursuing their callings because of their circumstances – rather they simply need to find part-time, responsible ways of doing this while still honoring their commitments. This path may involve established opportunities or require entrepreneurial approaches.

The Old Testament prophet Amos was one of these heroes. A farmer from Tekoa, Amos nonetheless answered the call of the LORD to bring his word to the people. The Apostle Paul was also an Extra-Curricular Path person, making and mending tents for his livelihood even while planting numerous churches and writing a third of the New Testament!

Earlier in this book, I mentioned my wife Pam and her labor of love, Providence Ranch Ministries. Pam is a mother of two growing boys, and continues to work part-time to contribute to the family income, all the while investing herself in area kids – thus, she is an example of The Extra-Curricular Path.

Let me illustrate other examples by listing well-known Extra-Curricular Path people along with an anonymous mix of those in my own church who amaze me everyday:

- A woman named Denise who, after completing her doctorate degree, chose to become a foster parent rather than immerse herself in the world of pure academia.
- An electrician named Rick who quietly mentors young men in their walk with Christ through a ministry called Strong Man.
- The lead singer of the Hall of Fame Rock band U2 named Bono. Rather than rest easy in the wealth and fame of his position, Bono has chosen instead to use his platform to be a Christian advocate for worldwide issues such as third world debt relief and AIDS.
- A retired couple, John and Monica, who devote significant amounts of their time to the local food shelter.
- The world famous software mogul, Bill Gates, and his wife Melinda, who through their foundation have raised and

directed billions of dollars toward third world health and education issues.

- A whole team of retired men who through their ministry called The Care Company, bless people who need basic carpentry work done in their homes.
- Jack, a local mechanic, who not only restores broken down automobiles, but also restores broken kids by inviting them into the process.

Honestly, I can't even begin to list them all.

These people are among my heroes. They are dangerous in all the right ways because they pursue their passion and calling in a way that honors the season of life which they find themselves in. The world is filled with such difference makers. History has been changed because of them.

So if you identify with this category, remember, your circumstances need not get in your way, they need only shape how you pursue your calling.

NEXT STEP:
Prayerfully use what you have (time, resources, etc.), start small and begin making a difference where you are.

The Explorer Path

If I'm right, there are a fair amount of readers who identify with this category. The temptation is to feel discouraged and frustrated that after all of the reading and assessment work, you feel no closer to your calling than when you started.

I understand ... really.

But believe it or not you have learned a lot about yourself, and you are closer. Sometimes the beginning of discovering who we are starts with discovering who we are not!

Your path may be the most exciting of all because the possibilities are all around you. But it will depend upon movement. In the words of TV personality Steve Harvey you will have to "jump."

(While addressing a Family Feud audience)

"Believe it or not, every successful person in this world has jumped. You cannot just exist in this life. You have got to try to live. If you are waking up thinking there has got to be more to your life than there is, man believe that it is. But to get to that life, you're gonna have to jump. ...

"You're gonna get an education, that's nice, but if you don't use your gift, that education's only gonna take you so far, I know a lot of people [who] got degrees man that ain't even using them. It's your gift. But the only way for you to soar is you got to jump. You got to take that gift that's packed away on your back, you got to jump off that cliff and pull that cord. That gift opens up and provides the soar. If you don't ever use it, you're gonna just go to work. And if you're getting up every day going to work on a job every day that you hate going to, that ain't living, man. You're just existing. At one point and time you outta see what living's like."[7]

The Explorer Path demands you to jump. Movement is essential. You will never discover God's calling and gifting in your life by standing still – by staring at your belly button. Part of what motivated me to write this book is my own experience with Christians who, after taking some sort of gift assessment, refuse to take action and jump into service claiming, "that area isn't my gift." What baloney.

"But jump where? In what direction?" You might be asking.

The beauty of your path is that the answer is simple:
Jump into any circumstance around you where there is need.

That's right. Jump toward the need. Meet the need. Even if you don't think it's your gifting.

---

7 | See Harvey's talk in its entirety on YouTube.

This is where your church has a significant role to play. Local bodies of believers, if they are obedient to Christ and alive in the Spirit in any way, will be able to point you to a myriad of needs:

- Sunday school teachers
- Nursery workers
- Youth program volunteers
- Musicians and worship tech people
- Greeters and ushers
- Mercy ministries in the local community (i.e. soup kitchens, food shelters, homeless shelters, non-profits, hospital visitation, pastoral care helpers, etc.)
- Hospitality ministries: Food preparation, funeral teams, etc.

Believe me, once you open yourself up to the various needs around you, you won't need to go looking for them, they will find you! It could be as simple as saying "yes" to leading your daughter's Girl Scout troop, or helping coach your son's soccer team.

You may think this sounds small or trivial, but it isn't. Adopt a servant's heart and meet the immediate need around you and I guarantee you God will be pleased. God honors servants who are willing to accept and be faithful in small things, by rewarding them with bigger things (remember Jesus' parable about the Talents, Matthew 25:14-30?).

You will be moving just the same as the other paths, you will just have a different starting point with a lot more possible roads to your destination. But remember, God himself will guide you – just be faithful, patient and observant. The first need you meet may, or may not, fit your gift mix. That's OK – just meet it faithfully. As you serve, God will begin to bring in different people and opportunities that will serve as signposts towards your calling. Follow the next best need or opportunity. Learn as you go. Stay close to the LORD in prayer and in his Word. You will be surprised at how faithful God is as your path takes shape, and your calling begins to emerge.

The Story of An Epic Explorer

This idea is illustrated beautifully in J.R.R Tolkien's *Lord of the Ring's* trilogy.

The story really starts when a small, seemingly insignificant hobbit named Frodo simply volunteers to carry a ring. It seems like such a little thing. He offers his help not realizing the full scope of what he will encounter. The ring is evil, and distorts the hearts of all who attempt to possess it. Carrying it becomes a burden to Frodo, and soon he realizes that this is his calling – even though the task is fraught with danger.

Frodo says "yes" to bearing the ring, but little does he know that in doing so, he would also scale mountains, flee demons, battle monsters, ride eagles, know the depths of betrayal, and the heights of true friendship. As the story ends, nothing less than the entire civilized world is saved because a seemingly inconsequential hobbit chooses to meet an immediate need.

As a new and hope-filled day dawns, Frodo, Sam, Merry, and Pippin are about to bow to the newly crowned King, Aragorn, but he stops them in front of everyone present and delivers one of the great lines of literature:

"My friends, you bow to no one."

The King bows to the hobbits instead, and the entire kingdom follows suit. The hobbits stand there and look around, surprised by this unexpected turn…and clearly a little unsure about being in such a lofty position.

Volumes could be written about this single scene: humility and exaltation, strength and faith conquering evil, the "last shall be first"…the themes are never-ending.

I am not trying to suggest that one day Jesus will bow down to you – but I am saying that one day he will say,

"Well done, good and faithful servant ..."[8]

Don't ever, ever think that your path is less significant than others.

You may not start out with as much certainty, but if you persevere you will end with much joy. Remember this verse we were first introduced to in Chapter One:

> *"Let us not become weary in doing good, for at the proper time we will reap a harvest if we do not give up."*
> **Galatians 6:9**

NEXT STEP:

Find an immediate need around you and meet it. Keep meeting needs; prayerfully paying attention to the people and opportunities God brings your way.

---

8 | Matthew 25:23

A Final Word From The Heart

Volumes have been written on the concept of God's calling and spiritual gifts. I confess to you that as I complete this book, the task was harder than I anticipated. You never really feel like you have said all there is to say ...

But maybe that is the point.

What I have shared with you is my small contribution to the ongoing conversation. It is gratefully built upon those who have gone before me in the hopes that others who come after will do the same. I offer it to you so that you might know Christ, know yourself, and begin the path God desires you to walk. I don't pretend in any way that I have covered everything there is to know on the subject. Others in the body of Christ will shed light on things I have missed or neglected. This is the beauty of how the body of Christ functions in the ongoing Kingdom of God.

I pray that if you have gotten to this point in the book, you have worked your way through all three parts. I pray that you have gained new and encouraging perspectives on scripture and the role of spiritual gifts. I pray that you have found the self-assessment thought-provoking and helpful. I pray that you have identified your Path; whether that is Entrepreneurial, Established, Extra-Curricular, or Explorer.

I hope you have not merely read this book. I hope you have wrestled with it. I hope you have understood that the point is not to engage in yet another spiritual version of belly-button staring.

I hope that in exploring your calling and gifts, you have come to the realization that it really isn't about you at all! I hope that you will take this reading and move beyond it ...and in so doing those around you will be blessed ... and Jesus will be known all the more.

Now ... get moving.

Jump.

About the Author

Randall J. Upgren (Randy) is Lead Pastor of Preaching and Teaching at Charity Lutheran Church, Bismarck, ND, where he has served since 1991. Charity is one of the largest churches in the LCMC and is known for its innovative approaches to ministry, including its highly popular WOW confirmation program.

Randy is a native to Bismarck, graduating from Bismarck High School (1985), and attaining his Associate's Degree in Music from Bismarck State College (1987) as a scholarship basketball athlete. Randy continued his education, graduating with a Bachelor's Degree in Music Industry from Moorhead State University, Minn. (1990). After being hired by Charity Lutheran Church as its first fill-time Director of Youth Ministries, Randy pursued further education, attaining his Master of Divinity Degree from Fuller Theological Seminary, Calif., in 2004.

Randy has been married to his wife, Pam, since 1993, and together they have two sons, Josh and Jordan. Pam has served as an Occupational Therapist at CHI - St. Alexius since 1990. Pam and Randy, as a team, established Providence Ranch Ministries, a nonprofit organization that seeks to use horses to mentor children from all walks of life, especially children dealing with various forms of disabilities. More information about Providence Ranch Ministries can be found at providenceranchnd.com. Randy is a sought-after speaker, addressing Christian and secular audiences alike on issues ranging from leadership, staff dynamics, Christian life and faith, popular culture from a Christian perspective and family and teen issues. His annul Teen Talk seminars in Bismarck/Mandan (since 2007) creatively minister to families seeking encouragement in the areas of teen sexuality, substance use and cultural pressures.

Randy can be reached to schedule an appearance on this book, or any of the aforementioned topics at randy.upgren@charitylutheran.org, or by calling 701-527-7983.